BLAISE PASCAL

THOUGHTS

BLAISE PASCAL
THOUGHTS

SELECTED AND TRANSLATED

BY

MORITZ KAUFMANN, M.A.

CAMBRIDGE UNIVERSITY PRESS
Cambridge, New York, Melbourne, Madrid, Cape Town,
Singapore, São Paulo, Delhi, Mexico City

Cambridge University Press
The Edinburgh Building, Cambridge CB2 8RU, UK

Published in the United States of America by Cambridge University Press, New York

www.cambridge.org
Information on this title: www.cambridge.org/9781107678033

First published 1908
First paperback edition 2013

A catalogue record for this publication is available from the British Library

ISBN 978-1-107-67803-3 Paperback

CONTENTS

CONTENTS

INTRODUCTION

BLAISE PASCAL, the author of the "Thoughts," was born at Clermont-Ferrand in Auvergne, June 19th, 1623. He belonged to an old legal family of distinction ; one of its members was ennobled by Louis XI. in 1478 for administrative services. His grandfather was treasurer of France, and his father, Etienne Pascal, was second president of the Court of Aides at Clermont, a man of considerable attainments, and the friend of most of the leading scientists and philosophers of his time. He relinquished his official post to devote himself entirely to the education of his son, who was in delicate health, but the child gave very early proofs of mathematical genius. His treatise on Conic Sections, written at the age of sixteen, excited the "mingled incredulity and astonishment" of Descartes. He was also the inventor of a calculating machine and ranks high among the scientific discoverers of that day. His religious experiences under the Jansenists date back to 1648, but his final or "definite" conversion took place in 1654, as the result of a miraculous escape from a serious carriage accident on the pont de Neuilly in Paris. The rest of his short life was spent mostly in pious seclusion and self-denying beneficence. As a temporary inmate of Port-Royal he engaged in controversy with the Jesuits and wrote the "immortal" Letters of a Provincial, and it was his intention to write an Apology of Christianity against Scepticism on similar lines. To this we owe the "Thoughts," a number of detached memoranda, jotted down from time to time as the materials for this work. Ill-health and an early death (he died August 19th, 1662) put an end to this plan, and the loose but mostly well-wrought-out thoughts, like so many clear-cut diamonds without a setting, remained in "the beautiful disorder" in which he left them until they were collected by his friends and published by them with alterations, additions, and omissions in 1670. The criticisms of V. Cousin published in 1842 pointed out the necessity of revision, and a restored text by M. Prosper-Faugère appeared in 1844.

Other editors, starting from different standpoints, have since then endeavoured to arrange and re-arrange the "Thoughts" in the order in which they suppose, from very insufficient data, that Pascal intended to place them. We follow that of M. Havet, as best adapted for an epitome of devotional reading in the present day.

Pascal, it should be remembered by those who make use of this manual, speaks with the authority of a scientific expert, as an original thinker, and profound student of human nature. Here we have a glimpse, so to speak, into the torture-chamber of his own mind, with its insatiable desire for spiritual enlightenment and intense love and pity for struggling humanity, anticipating in a curious way the perplexities of all those who think deeply and feel ardently in the pursuit of truth in our own day[1].

If his arguments, founded on Scripture proofs, prophecy, and miracles (considerably curtailed in the present selection), have lost some of their cogency with the progress of biblical criticism, his presentation of Christianity in its adaptation to human nature possesses still an undiminished value, heightened by the charm of his illuminating style, which unites elegance with almost geometrical precision and the playful ease of a man of the world with the concentration of religious ardour.

It is, however, the intellectual integrity of the

[1] On this the present writer ventures to refer to an article contributed by him to *The Quarterly Review* for April, 1906.

INTRODUCTION

"Thoughts" in their effort to reconcile thought and feeling by a fearless appeal to reason, and yet in a reverent spirit, which appeals so strongly to the spirit of our age. In their passionate earnestness in the search after truth they are calculated to stimulate and guide those who in the midst of modern difficulties surrounding religious speculation are ready to follow Pascal's exhortation *Croyez sciemment.* Seeing how he faced "the spectres of the mind," though less willing than he was to stifle doubt by the exaltation of faith, they will, perchance, endeavour, as one of his latest editors says, "to follow him from a distance to the solitary rock of high endeavour which forms one of the spiritual summits of humanity."

M. K.

August 10, 1908.

PASCAL'S THOUGHTS.

PART I.

THE MISERY OF MAN WITHOUT GOD.

A. MAN'S PLACE IN NATURE.

The Greatness and Littleness of Man.

LET man contemplate the whole realm of
nature in the light and fulness of her majesty;
let him withdraw his mind from the base objects
by which he is surrounded; let him fix his eye on
the brilliant light, placed like an everlasting lamp
to give light to the universe; then the Earth will
appear to him like a point in the vast circuit
described by this luminary. Let him stand and
wonder at the vast extent covered by its orbit,
itself a minute point compared with that described
by the stars revolving in the firmament. But
if our sight stops there, let imagination travel
beyond: he would sooner grow tired trying to
conceive than nature in furnishing him objects
for his sight. The whole of this visible universe
is only an imperceptible speck in the vast expanse

of nature. No, we can form no adequate idea of it. Vain are our efforts to extend our conceptions beyond all imaginable space, we produce but atoms in place of the reality of things. It is an infinite sphere, the centre of which is everywhere, the circumference nowhere. In fine, it is the most striking manifestation of Divine Omnipotence, overwhelming the imagination dwelling on it in thought. Then returning into himself let man consider what he is compared with the All; let him consider himself as a wanderer in this remote province of nature from the little dungeon in which he finds himself lodged, I mean the universe, let him learn to appraise himself at the true value.

What is man in the Infinite? But to bring before his mind another equally amazing prodigy, let him in his researches of what can be known examine what is most trifling. A mite in its tiny body displays parts of incomparable littleness, limbs with their joints, veins in those limbs, blood in these veins, humors in this blood, drops in these humors, vapours in these drops, so that, in subdividing these last still further, he will exhaust his powers of conception, until the least object he can descry shall be the subject of our discussion; he may then think perchance that he has reached the extreme point of littleness in nature. I will, then, open before him a new abyss,

THE INFINITELY GREAT AND LITTLE

I will paint for him not only the visible universe, but the immensity of nature as conceived by us within the limits of this epitome of an atom.

Let him see, then, an infinity of worlds, each having its own firmament, its planets, its earth, in due proportion as in the visible universe; in this Earth he will find animals down to mites in which he will find again the same characteristics, and yet in others, again, discovering the same thing in endless succession he will lose himself in these wonders, astounding alike in their smallness and greatness; for who can help wondering at our body but a little while ago imperceptible in the universe itself, imperceptible in the bosom of the whole, now become a colossus, a world, or rather a totality in respect to the nothingness beyond his grasp?

He who will give way to these considerations will be frightened at himself, and seeing himself suspended in the body nature has given him between these two abysses of the infinite and the nothing he will tremble at the sight of these marvels; and, I believe that, his curiosity changing into admiration, he will be more disposed to contemplate them in silence rather than in the spirit of presumptuous research.

For, after all, what is man in nature? nothing in respect of infinity, everything in respect of non-existence, placed midway between nothing and everything. Infinitely removed from understanding the extremes, the finality of things and their beginnings invincibly hidden from him in impenetrable mystery; equally incapable of seeing the nothing whence he came in the first instance, and the infinite in which he is ingulfed.

What, then, will he do unless it be to discern what appears to be the middle of things, in a sempiternal despair of ever knowing either their beginning or their end? All things have come from nothing and are borne on to infinity. Who will trace this astonishing march? The author of these marvels understands them, no one else can.

Not having considered these infinites men have set themselves with temerity to investigate nature, as if they bore some proportion to her.

It is a strange thing this wish of theirs to understand the principle of things and thence to arrive at complete knowledge with a presumption as infinite as the object matter. For without doubt one cannot entertain such a design without a presumption, or a capacity like that of nature herself.

*   *   *   *   *   *

Let us understand, then, our own limitation; we are something, but we are not everything, our mode of existence hides from us the knowledge of

4

first principles which spring from the nothing, and the littleness of our being hides from our view the infinite.

Our intelligence holds the same place in the realm of thought that our body occupies in the whole range of natural existence.

In every way limited this position of occupying the mean between two extremities turns up in all our infirmities, our senses are incapable of perceiving extremes. Too much noise deafens us; too much light dazzles; extreme distance, or propinquity impedes sight; excessive length, or brevity in speech renders it obscure; too much truth appals. I know of some, who cannot understand that to subtract four from nothing leaves nought. First principles appear to us too self-evident; too much pleasure proves irksome; too much harmony in music proves unpleasant; too many acts of kindness have an irritating effect. We like to have the means of paying over and above that we owe, " Beneficia eo usque laeta sunt dum videntur exsolvi posse; ubi multum antevenere, pro grata odium redditur." We feel neither extreme heat, nor extreme cold. Qualities in excess are repugnant to our nature and leave us insensible. We do not feel, we simply endure them. Too much virility and too much senility are an impediment to the spirit, as

5

also too much, and too little instruction. In fine, extreme things are for us as if they did not exist, nor in regard to these have we existence, they escape us, and we them.

This, then, is our true state. This renders us incapable of certain knowledge and of absolute ignorance. We float in a vast medium, ever uncertain and fluctuating, pushed from end to end. Any point to which we thought of attaching ourselves firmly gives way and fails us, and if we try to follow it up it will elude our grasp, flitting away a fugitive for ever. Nothing stays for us. This is our natural state, and, at all times, most contrary to our inclination. We are aflame with desire to find a firm sediment, an ultimate, fixed basis on which to build a tower which shall reach the infinite. But our whole foundation cracks and the ground beneath opens up the abyss.

Let us, then, cease from seeking assurance and stability. Our reason is at all times deceived by the shifting appearance of things. Nothing can fix the finite between the two infinites which enclose and fly from it.

This being understood we may rest satisfied each in the place where nature has placed us. This place assigned us as our lot, being always distant from both extremes, what does it matter if man has a trifle more knowledge of things? His possession only carries him a little higher. Is he not always infinitely distant from the end, and the duration of our life is it not at an equally infinite distance from eternity though it last ten years longer?

In view of these infinities, all finites are equal; nor do I see why he should let his imagination rest on one more than the other. The only comparison we can make of ourselves in our finite condition is accompanied by pain.

If man began by studying himself he would see how impotent he is to get beyond this; how impossible it is that a part should know the whole. But he may aspire to know at least those parts to which he bears some proportionate relation. But the parts in this world are so related and linked to one another that I consider it impossible to know one without the other, and without the whole.

Man, for example, is related to all that he knows. He requires space to contain him, time to exist in, movement to live in, the elements of which he is composed, heat and nourishment to sustain him, air to breathe. He sees the light, he feels bodies,—in short everything enters the blend of his being.

To know man, therefore, it is necessary to discover why he wants air to subsist in, and to know what air is he must know in what way it is related to human life, &c.

7

Flame cannot exist without air: therefore to know the one we must know the other. All things, then, being either cause or effect, supporting, or receiving support, mediate, or immediate, and all things being held together by a natural and imperceptible link, joining those that are most distant and dissimilar, I hold that it is as impossible to know the parts without knowing the whole as it is to know the whole without detailed knowledge of the parts. What completes our impotence of the knowledge of things is the fact that they are simple in themselves, whereas we are composed of two heterogeneous natures different in kind, of soul and body; for it is impossible that the reasonable faculty can be anything but spiritual; and if any one were to assert that we consist of body alone this would preclude still more the knowledge of things, as there is nothing more inconceivable than to say that matter knows itself. It is impossible for us to know how it could know itself. And thus if we are simply material we can know nothing at all, and if we are composed of mind and matter we cannot know perfectly simple substances, whether they are corporeal or spiritual.

Hence it is that nearly all the philosophers confuse the ideas of things and speak of bodily things in terms of mind, and of spiritual things in terms of body. For they boldly assert that bodies tend downwards, that they are attracted towards the centre, that they fly from destruction, that nature abhors a vacuum and has inclinations, sympathies, antipathies, all things which belong to the spirit exclusively. Again, in speaking of spirits they think of them in a fixed locality, or as moving from place to place, qualities which belong to bodies only.

Instead of receiving ideas of things as they are we tinge with qualities of our composite nature all the simple things we contemplate.

Who would not think, seeing us mixing up matter with mind in everything, that such a compound would be easily understood by us? Yet this is the least comprehensible thing of all. To himself man appears the most formidable object in nature; for he is unable to conceive what is body, and still less what is mind, and least of all how body and mind can be united. Here is the crown of all his difficulties and yet this constitutes the very nature of his being. *Modus quo corporibus adhaerent spiritus comprehendi ab hominibus non potest, et hoc tamen homo est.*

The greatness of man consists in the grandeur of knowing himself to be miserable. A tree has no sense of its misery. True, it is misery to know ourselves to be miserable; but it is a grand thing, too, that he is miserable. These very miseries prove his grandeur. They are the miseries of a great nobleman, the miseries of a discrowned king.

For who finds himself miserable for not being king but he who has been dispossessed of his kingdom? Was Paulus Emilius considered unhappy because he ceased to be consul? On the contrary, everybody knew him to be happy for having been one as it was in the nature of things to be so for a time. But Perseus was known to be unhappy because he ceased to be king, in his case it was natural to be always king; so that it seemed strange that he could endure life. Who considers himself unhappy for having no more than one mouth? But who would not feel unhappy in having only one eye? One could not feel distressed for want of three eyes, but one would be unconsolable in possessing none at all. We have such a high idea of the human mind that we cannot bear its contempt or to be deprived of its esteem; and all human happiness consists in the enjoyment of this esteem....

And those who despise men most and rank them among the beasts still wish to be admired and trusted and are in contradiction with themselves by their own feelings, nature, which is stronger than all else, convincing them of the greatness of man with greater force than their reason can convince them of his baseness.

Man is but a reed, the feeblest in nature, but he is a reed that thinks. It needs not that the whole universe should arm itself to crush him; a vapour, a drop of water suffices to kill him. But should the universe crush him, man would still be more noble than his destroyer, because he knows that he dies and the advantage the universe has over him. The universe knows nothing of the kind.

All our dignity, then, consists in thought. By this we must raise ourselves, not by space and time which we could not fill. Let us try, then, to think aright, here is the foundation of morality.

It is not in space that I must look for any dignity, but in regulated thought. The possession of worlds will not add to it. In space the universe encompasses, swallows me up like a point; by thought I comprehend it. It is a dangerous thing to make man see that he is on a level with the beasts without showing him his grandeur, and still more dangerous to make him see his grandeur without his baseness.

More dangerous still it is to let him overlook one or the other. But it is of great advantage to make him acquainted with both.

It is unnecessary for man to believe himself

equal to the beasts, or equal to the angels, nor should he be ignorant of either one or the other, but he should know both.

Let man form an estimate of his proper value. Let him love himself, for he has a nature capable of good, but let him not on this account love the baseness which adheres to it. Let him despise himself because this capacity is ineffective, but let him not on that account despise the natural capacity itself. Let him hate himself, love himself, for he has the capacity to know the truth and to be happy; but he possesses no truth which is either constant, or complete. I would, therefore, get man to have a desire to find it, to be ready, freed from passions, to follow its guidance when he has found it, knowing to what extent his knowledge is obscured by the passions; I would that he contest those corrupt desires by force of which his conduct is determined, that they may not blind him in making his choice, nor frustrate that choice when he has made it.

The Stoics say: Retire into yourselves, then you will find rest. But this is not true. Others say: Go out of yourselves! look for happiness in amusement. This, too, is untrue; sickness sets in. Happiness is not to be found either without, or within, it is in God, both within and without ourselves.

TWO VIEWS OF MAN'S NATURE

Man's nature may be considered in two ways, one according to its end, then it is grand and incomparable; the other according to public opinion, as one judges of the nature of a horse or a dog, seeing how they run, *et animum arcendi*; in that case man is abject and vile. These are the two ways leading to different judgments and cause disputes among philosophers. For one denies the premises of the other. One says man was not born for this end, for all his actions are opposed to it; the other says he turns away from the end in view when he is guilty of these base actions.

Two things give man a complete knowledge of his nature, instinct and experience. I can understand the possibility of not having existed: for the *ego* consists in my thought; hence I, this thinking being, would never have existed if my mother had been killed before I began to live. Therefore there is no necessity for my existence. Nor am I eternal or infinite; yet I can see well enough that there is in nature a necessary being, eternal and infinite.

Man's Vanity and Self-love.

We are not content with the possession of life such as it is in our present condition: we desire an imaginary life in the ideas of others and try our best to save appearances. We try incessantly to embellish and preserve this imaginary being, and neglect the real one. And if we possess tranquillity, or generosity, or fidelity, we are eager to let it be known that we may attach these virtues to this creature of our imagination. We would rather part with them for this end and gladly become cowards if thereby we could acquire the reputation for valour. This is a remarkable proof of the nothingness of our real life not to be satisfied with it without the other, and often to renounce it for the other! For he who would not die to preserve his honour, would be contemptible.

Such is our delight with this glory that with whatever it is combined, even death itself, we still love it.

Pride is a counterpoise to all our miseries; we either conceal, or display them, when we pride ourselves on our knowledge of them. Pride has a natural hold of us in all our miseries, errors, &c. We even give up life cheerfully, provided people talk of it.

Vanity is anchored in the human heart to such an extent that a soldier, common labourer, a cook, a porter boasts and wants to have his admirers: even philosophers are anxious for them. And those who write against it yearn for the glory of having well written; and those who read it want to have the glory of having read it; and I, who write this, perhaps have the same desire, and perhaps those who will read it....

Even in the presence of all the miseries which press upon us, and take us by the throat, we have an irrepressible instinct which lifts us up.

We are so presumptuous that we could wish to be known all over the world even by those who will come after us when we are gone, and we are so vain that the esteem of five or six persons about us affords us amusement and content.

Curiosity is nothing else but vanity. In most instances we only want to know so as to talk about it. Otherwise we should not cross the sea if it were not to speak of it, but simply for the pleasure of seeing without the hope of telling others about it.

The essence of self-love in man, this human *ego*, is only to love and consider oneself. But what can it do? It cannot prevent the object so loved being full of faults and miseries. Man wants to be great and sees that he is little; he wants to be happy and feels himself miserable; he wants to be perfect and sees himself full of imperfection; he wants to be the object of man's love and esteem and sees that his faults only deserve their aversion and contempt. This embarrassment wherein he finds himself produces the most un-

15

justifiable and criminal passion imaginable; for he feels a mortal hatred for this truth which reproves and convicts him of shortcomings. He would like to annihilate it, and, not being able to destroy it in its essence, he does so as far as possible in keeping the knowledge of it away from himself and others: that is to say he does all he can to hide his faults from others and himself, and cannot bear that either he or they should see them.

It is undoubtedly an evil to be full of faults, but it is a greater evil still to be full of them and not to be willing to recognise them since it adds another fault, that of voluntary illusion. We do not like others to deceive us; we do not consider it just on their part to require us to esteem them beyond their desert; it is equally unjust that we should deceive them, and that we want them to esteem us more than we deserve.

Thus when they discover only those imperfections and vices which are really part of ourselves, it is plain that they do us no wrong at all, since it is not they who are the cause of them; that they actually confer on us a benefit in enabling us to get rid of an evil, that is the ignorance of our defects. We ought not to be annoyed at their knowing them and despising us, since it is but just that they should know us for

16

what we are and despise us if we are despicable. Such would be the feeling arising in a heart full of equity and justice. What then shall we say of ours in finding there a disposition quite different from this? For is it not a fact that we hate the truth and those who tell it us and that we like them to be deceived in our favour and that we want to be esteemed by them as being different from what we really are?

Here is a proof inspiring me with horror. The Catholic religion does not oblige us to make known our sins indiscriminately to the world at large : it permits us to keep our secret from others, but there is one person before whom it requires us to lay bare the bottom of our heart to show ourselves to him as we are. There is only this one man in the world whom she orders us to undeceive, and he is bound to inviolable secrecy so that this knowledge to him is as if it did not exist. Can anything be imagined more charitable and lenient? Yet such is the corruption of man that he even finds this obligation to be a hardship, so that it is one of the chief reasons of revolt against the Church in a large portion of Europe.

How unreasonable and unjust is the human heart to consider it a bad thing to have to do towards one man that which in a way is due to all! For is it right to deceive them?

There are different degrees of this aversion to truth, but to some degree, it may be said, it is to be found in all as it is inseparable from self-love. Hence that false delicacy which obliges those who have to reprimand others to select indirect methods and modifications so as to avoid giving offence. They are bound to extenuate our faults, to affect to excuse them, mingling them with praises and assurances of affection and esteem. Yet all this does not prevent the medicine tasting bitter to self-love. It takes as little of it as possible and always with disgust and sometimes with a secret spite against those who administer it.

Hence it comes that those whose interest it is to be liked by us avoid rendering us a service which they know will prove disagreeable, they treat us as we like to be treated: we hate the truth so they hide it from us; we want to be flattered and they flatter us; we like to be deceived and they deceive us.

The result is that every step in advance in good fortune, raising us in the world, removes us further still from the truth, because people are afraid of offending those whose affection is as useful as their dislike is dangerous. A prince may thus become the talk of all Europe, and be the only person who does not know it. I am not astonished at this: to speak the truth is useful to him to whom it is spoken, but disadvantageous to those who tell it, for they incur hatred in consequence. But those who consort with princes prefer their own interest to that of the prince they serve and hence they do not care to be of benefit to him if it be to their own hurt.

This evil is undoubtedly more formidable and more common in the most highly placed, but those in the lower rank are not exempt from it, for there is always some object to be gained in getting into the good graces of others. Thus human life is nothing but perpetual illusion ; people never cease flattering and deceiving each other. None speak of us when we are present in the same way as when we are absent. The union which exists among men is solely founded on mutual deception ; few friendships would survive if each knew what his friend says of him in his absence, though he may be speaking of him sincerely and without passion.

Man, then, is nothing but a creature of disguises, falsehoods, and hypocrisy, both towards himself and others. He does not want to hear the truth, he avoids speaking it to others, and all these tendencies thus far removed from justice and reason have their natural root in his heart.

Man's Feebleness and Ignorance—Imagination the Mistress of Error.

What astonishes me more than anything is to see that the world of human beings is not astonished at its weakness. People go on in all seriousness, each attending to his own mode of life, not because it is really good to follow it, but in deference to the general habit, as if each knew for certain the path of reason and justice. Men are constantly deceived, but by a kind of absurd humility they suppose that it is their own fault and not that of the art they always pride themselves of possessing. But it is well that there should be so many people of this sort in the world, who are not sceptics for the glory of scepticism, but to show that man is quite capable of the most extravagant notions, since he is capable of believing that he is not in this natural and inevitable state of weakness, but, on the contrary, in the possession of natural wisdom.

Nothing props up scepticism so much as the fact that there are some who are not sceptics; if they all were so, they would be wrong.

Imagination, this mistress of error and falsehood, is that part of man which deceives him and all the more treacherous in not being so invariably; for it would be an infallible rule of truth if it were an infallible rule of falsehood. But being for the most part fallacious it cannot be clearly distinguished, having both the characteristics of truth and falsehood. I do not speak of fools, but of the wisest of men; it is among them that imagination has the greatest power of persuasion. In vain cries out reason, it cannot appraise things at their true value.

This arrogant power, the enemy of reason, taking delight in controlling and domineering over it, has created a second nature in man to demonstrate its universal sway. She has her happy and unhappy subjects, healthy or sick, wealthy or poor; she compels reason to believe, doubt and deny; she causes a suspense of real by substituting factitious sentiment; she has her own fools and sages and nothing vexes us more than seeing how she fills her pensioners with a satisfaction far more perfect and complete than does reason. Those who have a vivid imagination feel a greater complacency than the discreet, who can only be pleased with themselves in a reasonable manner. The former look on people with a sense of mastery; they argue with hardihood and self-confidence whilst the latter do so with fear and diffidence: and this gaiety of countenance gives them often an advantage in the opinion of their audience insomuch that the wise in their own imagination enjoy the favour of judges of a similar character. Imagination cannot turn wise men into fools, but it can make the fools happy in spite of reason, which can only make her friends miserable; the one covers them with glory, the other with shame.

Who is this dispenser of reputation, which bestows respect, and veneration on persons, works, laws and the great, but this faculty of imagination? How unsatisfactory the wealth in the universe would be but for her assent?

Would you not say that yonder magistrate whose venerable age inspires universal respect is governed by pure and lofty reason, that he judges all causes according to their true nature, unaffected by those trivial circumstances which only affect the imagination of the weak? See him go to sermon full of devout zeal, enforcing the equanimity and solidity of reason with the ardour of charity! He is prepared to listen to it with exemplary respect. Let the preacher appear to whom nature has given a husky voice, a funny expression of face, or whose barber has shaved him badly by chance ; in addition let his clothes be splashed; I lay a wager the gravity of our venerable senator will be upset though the truths preached be ever so weighty.

The greatest philosopher in the world walking across a plank broader than need be, if there is a precipice below, though assured by reason of his safety, will be overpowered by his imagination. Few could bear the thought of it without a cold sweat, or growing pale.

It is a well known fact that the sight of cats, of rats, or the crushing of a bit of coal will put some persons out of their wits ; the tone of a voice imposes on the wisest, and alters the effect of a speech or a poem. Affection or dislike changes the face of justice ; and more than one advocate paid in advance finds the cause he pleads for more just in consequence ! His confident air produces a more favourable impression on the judges, who are taken in by this appearance ; a fine sort of reason that which is swayed by a breath of wind in every direction !

Our magistrates are fully aware of this secret. Their scarlet robes, and ermine, in which they wrap themselves like furred cats, the halls in which they administer justice, the fleurs de lis, all this imposing array has its importance, and if doctors had not their gowns and mules, and the learned in the law their square caps and robes four times the size required, they would never have imposed upon the world, which cannot resist the effect of this show of authority. Soldiers are the only class of people who do not require this kind of mummery because in effect their part is more real. They establish themselves by a real power, others by feigning it.

For this reason our kings have no need of resorting to disguises like these, or masquerading in strange attire to appear such, yet they are surrounded by guards and halberds, these red-faced men in armour, whose hands of force exist for them alone ; these trumpets and drums, marching in front of them, these legions surrounding their person send a tremor through the firmest minds. They do not only wear the uniform, but possess the power. It needs a high degree of pure reason to regard him, who is surrounded in his superb seraglio by four thousand janissaries, as anything else but a great potentate.

If magistrates had true justice, and if our doctors possessed the true art of healing, there would be no need for their square caps, the majesty of superior knowledge would render them sufficiently venerable. But having only imaginary learning they must perforce use these inane artifices to impress the imagination where it is necessary and thereby in fact to secure respect.

We cannot look at an advocate arrayed in wig and gown without entertaining a more favourable opinion of his capacity. Imagination rules everything. It creates beauty, justice, happiness which embrace everything the world holds. I should be glad to see the Italian book of which I only know the title, which in itself is of more value than many books : *Della opinione regina del mondo* (Opinion, Queen of the world). I endorse its sentiments without knowing its contents barring the evil that may be found there.

Here you have, as near as possible, the effects of this deceptive faculty which seems to have been given to us for the express purpose to lead inevitably into error. There are, however, many other sources of the same error.

Not only old impressions are able to lead us astray ; the charms of novelty have the same power. Hence arise all the disputes among men, either reproaching each other for following the erroneous impressions of childhood, or running too rashly after novelties. Who keeps to the just middle? Let him come forward and prove it ! There is no principle be it ever so natural, though dating from our earliest childhood, which may not be represented as a false impression produced by education or the senses. Some one may say : " Simply because from childhood you have believed that a trunk is empty when you see nothing in it, you have believed in the possibility of a vacuum, it is an illusion of your senses, strengthened by habit, which science must correct." Others say because they taught you in school that there is no vacuum your common sense has been imposed upon, which understood it well enough before this false impression; therefore there is need for correction by a return to primitive nature. Who, then, was the deceiver? Sense or Education? There is another element of error, our illnesses; they impair the judgment and the senses, and if the graver maladies make a considerable alteration, I doubt not that minor ailments make their impression, too, in proportion.

Our self-interest, moreover, is a wonderful instrument in warping our views to our own satisfaction. It is not given to the most impartial man to be a proper judge in his own case. There are some, I know, who, in order not to fall under the influence of this self-love, have been most egregiously unjust in the opposite direction. With such the surest way to ruin an entirely just cause, is to have it recommended to them by one of their own relatives. Justice and truth are two points so subtle, that our instruments are too blunt to touch them with nicety; if they succeed they crush the point, or lean all round it, more on the false than the true.

The chancellor is grave and covered with ornamental attire, for he is in a false position;

not so the king, he has the real power and has nothing to do with imagination. Judges, doctors, &c., have nothing but this to fall back upon.

The most important thing affecting the whole life is the choice of a profession : yet chance determines it. It is custom that makes masons, soldiers, thatchers. People say he is an excellent thatcher, and in speaking of soldiers : What big fools they are ! Others, on the contrary, will say : There is nothing so noble as the profession of arms, all the rest are good for nothing. Being accustomed to hear some of these callings praised when we are young, and others despised, we make our choice accordingly. For we naturally love truth and hate folly. Then words move us : our only fault is in the application. So great is the power of custom that of those, whom nature has only made men, we make men of various conditions; some localities only produce masons, others soldiers, &c. Nature, doubtless, is not uniform in her products. It is custom which brings this about, for it puts a constraint on nature; sometimes nature gets the upper hand and keeps men back to follow their own instinct in spite of custom, good or bad.

We never confine ourselves to the present. We anticipate the future, too slow in coming, as if to accelerate its course ; or we recall the past in eluding too fast, to slacken its pace: so inconsiderate are we that we wander about in the times which are not our own, and give no thought to the only part of it which is at our disposal; and we are so foolish that we dwell on that which exists no longer, whilst that which still remains escapes our attention. For as generally the present gives us pain, we put it out of sight because it distresses us; and if it is pleasant, we regret to see it escape. We try to support it by (thought of) the future, and think we can dispose of the things which are beyond our power towards the time of which we are not sure that it will come. Let anybody examine his thoughts and he will find that they are occupied entirely with the past and the future. We scarcely ever think of the present, and if we think of it, this is only as a means to light the way in preparing for the future. The present is never the end in view. The past and present are our means, the future alone is the end. Thus we never live, but hope to live; and whilst we are always getting ready to be happy it is inevitable that we never are so.

Our imagination exaggerates so much the life that now is, in compelling us to give it constant thought, that we make nothing of eternity for want of reflection, and an eternity of nothing.

All this has its vital roots in ourselves so that no effort of reason can prevent it.

Cromwell was about to overturn the whole of Christendom; the royal family was lost and his own permanently established but for a small grain of sand. Rome herself was ready to tremble before him, but this little bit of gravel, being placed in his bladder, he died, his family became abused, all ends in peace and the king being restored.

On what shall man found the economy of the world he wants to govern? Is it on the caprice of each individual? What confusion! Is it upon justice? We know nothing about it.

Certainly if men knew it, they would not have established the maxim most generally accepted among men, that each must follow the custom of his country. The glory of true equity would have brought all people under its sway, and legislators would not have taken for their model the fancies and caprices of Persians and Germans, or Indians in the place of this immutable justice. We should have seen it established in all states, in all times, whereas we do not see either justice, or injustice, which does not change its quality with a change of climate. Three degrees of latitude reverse all jurisprudence. A meridian decides what is truth, after a few years of possession fundamental laws

change, right has its epochs. The entrance of
Saturn into Lion marks for us the origin of such
and such a crime. Fine justice that which is
bounded by a river! It is truth on this side of
the Pyrenees, and error on that.

It is admitted that justice does not consist in
these customs, but that it resides in the laws of
nature as understood all over the world. They
would certainly maintain it obstinately if rash
chance, the disseminator of human laws, had
encountered one at least which was universal: but
the mocking of this human caprice is so diverse
that there is none.

Theft, incest, child-murder, and parricide—all
these have been numbered among virtuous actions.
Can there be anything more absurd than a man
should have a right to kill me because he lives
on the other side of the water, or because his
prince has a quarrel with mine, though I have no
quarrel with him?

No doubt there are natural laws, but this
fair reason, corrupt in itself, corrupts everything.
*Nihil amplius nostrum est; quod nostrum dicimus,
artis est. Ex senatusconsultis et plebiscitis cri-
mina exercentur. Ut olim vitiis, sic nunc legibus
laboramus.*

Owing to this confusion one says that the
essence of justice is the authority of the legislator;

another, the conscience of the ruler; another, the prevailing custom, and the last is the safest: according to reason nothing is just in itself. All yields to time; custom alone is the creator of equity for the simple reason that this is accepted. This forms the hidden foundation of its authority. He who tries to trace it to its first principles annihilates it. Nothing is so faulty as those laws which redress faults; he who obeys them on account of their justice obeys an imaginary justice, not the essential principle of law. This is wholly concentrated in itself. It is law and nought else. He who tries to examine the main spring will find it so slight and feeble, that if he is in the habit of contemplating the eccentricities of human imagination he will wonder that a single age could procure for it so much homage and veneration. The art of shaking and overthrowing states is to disturb established customs in tracing them to their source, to point out their lack of authority and justice. We must, say they, go back to the fundamental and original laws of the realm which illegal usage has abolished. This is a game certain to result in loss of all; nothing will be just under this scrutiny. Yet the people lend no willing ear to this kind of discussion. They break the yoke as soon as they recognise its nature, and those in power profit by its ruin and the ruin of the curious enquirers into the foundation of received customs and fundamental laws of a past age. Yet by a contrary defect men sometimes fancy that they may justly do everything which is without precedent. For this reason the wisest of lawgivers said that it was often necessary to dupe mankind for their own good, and another able politician affirms : *Quum veritatem, qua liberetur, ignoret, expedit quo fallatur.* Man must not be made to feel the truth about usurpation ; it was once introduced without reason, it became reasonable ; it must now be regarded as authoritative, immutable, and its beginning must be concealed if we do not wish that it should come to a speedy end.

The mind of this sovereign judge of the universe is not so independent that it is not liable to be disturbed by the first din about it. It needs not the report of the cannon to break the train of thought ; the creaking of a vane, or of a pulley will do it. Do not feel astonished if he does not reason well at this moment ; a fly is buzzing near his ears. This suffices to render him incapable of sound judgment. If you want to put him in the way of finding the truth, drive away the insect which keeps his reason in check and troubles this powerful intellect which governs cities and kingdoms. A fine god that ! *O ridicolissimo Eroe!*

WILL AS A DETERMINING FACTOR

There is a universal and essential difference between actions of the will and all other actions.

Will is one of the principal organs of belief, not that it forms belief, but that things are true, or false according to the view we take of them. The will, which prefers one to the other, diverts the mind from considering the qualities of all it does not like to see: thus the mind going some distance with the will stays to look at the side it likes and so judges by what it sees.

Imagination exaggerates small things until they fill our soul with a fantastic estimate and by a rash insolence belittles the great by its own measure, as when it speaks of God.

All the pursuits of men are for the purpose of acquiring wealth, yet they cannot have a tittle to possess it with justice, but only human fancy, nor have they the power to hold it securely. So it is with science, illness deprives men of it. We are incapable both of truth and goodness.

What are our natural principles but those of custom, and among children those received from the habits of their fathers as predatory habits in lower animals? Difference of custom will give rise to other natural principles. This is seen by experience; and if there are some ineffaceable by habit there are also others contrary to nature, which are ineffaceable by nature, or acquired habit. This defends a disposition.

Fathers are afraid lest the natural love of children should be extinguished. What kind of nature is this, then, which is liable to be effaced? Habit, then, is a second nature which destroys the first. But what is nature? Why is habit not natural? I am very much afraid that nature is itself but primary habit, as habit is second nature.

If night after night we dreamed the same it would affect us as much as the things we see by day; and if an artisan were to dream every night for twelve hours that he was a king, I think he would be nearly as happy as a king who should dream that he was an artisan.

If we dreamed every night that we are pursued by enemies, disturbed by these painful phantoms, and that at the same time our days were passed in diverse pursuits, as in travelling, we should suffer almost as much as if the dream were real, and we should dread to go to sleep just as we dread the awaking when there is the fear of incurring such misfortunes in reality. In fact it would produce nearly the same evils as the reality. But because dreams differ, and a single one even assumes different shapes, that which we see in them affects us much less than what we see when awake, for then there is continuity, though

34

that is not level and persistent so as to be immutable, but less abrupt except rarely as when we are travelling, and then we say: "It seems to me, I am dreaming," for life is a sleep only a little less constant. We imagine that all look at things in the same way; but it is a gratuitous supposition of which we have no proof whatever. I see plainly that we use the same words on the same occasions, that each time two persons see a body changing its position, both express the same thing in the same words, saying one to the other, "it has moved"; and from this conformity in the application of terms a strong presumption arises of a conformity of ideas; but this is by no means absolutely and finally convincing, though there is enough for a wager to favour the affirmative; since we know that often the same consequences are deduced from different premises.

It is enough, at least, to confuse the matter. Not that it absolutely destroys the natural light, which makes us sure of these things: the men of the Academy would have the advantage; but it obscures it, and troubles the dogmatists to the glory of the Pyrrhonic Cabal, which rests on this ambiguous ambiguity, and in a certain state of doubtful obscurity from which our doubts cannot take away all the light nor our natural light banish all the darkness.

The world judges well of many things, for it is in a state of natural ignorance which is the true wisdom of man. The sciences have two extremes which touch each other. The first is the pure natural ignorance in which all men are born. The second is that at which great men arrive when after having run through the whole circle of human knowledge they find that they know nothing, and that they are face to face with the same ignorance from which they started. But this is a wise ignorance which knows itself. But those between the two, who have started from the first but have not arrived at the second, have a certain tincture of learned self-sufficiency and pose as those who know.

These disturb the world and judge ill of all things. The people and the really clever persons make up the world generally; these despise it and are despised, they judge ill of all things and the world judges rightly of them.

Man is a subject full of natural error which is ineradicable, without grace. Nothing shows him the truth: everything deceives him. These two principles of truth, reason and the senses, apart from the fact that they both are wanting in sincerity, deceive each other. The senses deceive the judgment by false appearances; and this same trickery they apply to reason, they are sub-

36

jected in return to the same trickery on the part of reason. Passions trouble our senses and impart to them false impressions. They are vying with each other in lying and deceit.

Man's Misery, producing Restlessness and Distraction.

We burden men from their infancy with the care of their honour, property, and friends, and also of the property and honour of their friends. We load them with business, the study of languages and bodily exercises and give them to understand that, unless their health, honour, and fortune and those of their friends were in good condition they would not be happy and that the lack of even one thing would render them unhappy. Thus we force them into tasks and occupations which harass them. A strange way, you will say, of securing their happiness! What more could be done to render them miserable? How now! what could be done? You have but to relieve them of all these cares; for then they could see themselves, they would think about themselves, what they are, whence they come, whither they go, and thus one cannot occupy or divert them too much. And for this reason, after having provided them with so much business, if there be any time for relaxation, they are advised to employ it in play and diversion so as to be always fully occupied.

When I set myself upon occasion to consider the different causes of agitation among men, the perils and toils to which they expose themselves in the court, and in the camp, the sources of so many quarrels, passions, dangerous and criminal enterprises, I discovered that the cause of all man's misfortune consists in this one thing, his inability to remain quietly in one room. A man who has enough to live on if he knew what a pleasure it is to remain at home would not set out to cross the sea, or join a siege. People would not buy an expensive commission in the army were it not that they find it insupportable never to budge from the town; they look for conversation and diversion in play simply because they cannot find any pleasure in remaining at home.

But when I considered the matter more closely, and after having discovered the cause of all our miseries, I tried to find a reason for it; I found that there is one most efficient cause, which consists in the natural unhappiness of our feeble and mortal condition, so that nothing can console us if we consider it with close attention.

Imagine a condition in which are united all

38

the good things we are capable of possessing, surely royalty is the finest position in the world, and yet suppose a king surrounded by all that is capable of giving him satisfaction; if he be left without diversion, at liberty to consider and reflect upon his own existence, this languid felicity will not sustain him; he will begin to dwell on the maladies which threaten him, possible revolts and at last death and such diseases as are inevitable; so that if he be deprived of what people call amusement, behold him miserable, and more so than the least of his subjects, who plays and amuses himself:

Hence it is that play, the society of ladies, war, and high offices are so much sought after. It is not that there is actually any happiness in these, or that any one imagines that real bliss consists in having money which can be won in gambling, in the hare you hunt; you would not have these as a gift. We care not for the easy and peaceable mode of life, which leaves us free to think about our sad condition, neither for dangers in war, nor cares of office, but the distraction, which turns us away and diverts the mind from dwelling on itself. (This is the reason why we prefer pursuit to possession.)

Hence it is that men are so fond of bustle and movement; hence it is that the prison is such a dreadful punishment; hence it is that the pleasure of solitude is so little understood. And finally, the greatest subject of felicity in the condition of kings is, that all about them incessantly try to divert them and procure for them all sorts of pleasures.

The king is surrounded by people whose only object it is to amuse him and to prevent him thinking about himself. For he is miserable, though he is a king, if he thinks about himself.

This is all human beings have been able to devise in order to secure their own happiness. And those who pose as philosophers in this matter, and think that the rest of the world is irrational in passing whole days in running after the hare they would not think worth buying, know nothing of human nature. The hare cannot screen us from the sight of death and our miseries, but chasing him does it. And thus, if we were to reproach them for seeking with so much ardour what can yield no satisfaction, and they replied, as they would do, that in this they only seek a violent impetuous activity to keep thought off from themselves and that for this reason they find in it the desirable object that charms and ardently attracts them, they would leave their adversaries without reply. But this is not the answer they give, because they do not know themselves; they are unaware that it is only the chase, and not the game taken, which they care for.

They imagine that if they but obtained this or that office they could settle down quietly with pleasure, and do not perceive that it is in the nature of desire to be insatiable. They think that they are looking for rest in all sincerity, whilst really they seek nothing else but distraction.

A secret instinct makes them look for diversion and occupation outside themselves, which arises from a feeling of their continual misery; and they have another secret instinct, a relic of the grandeur of their original condition, which teaches them that happiness is in effect only found in rest, not in tumult, and between these two contrary instincts there arises a confused plan, hidden from their view, in the depth of their soul, which leads them to seek repose through agitation and constantly to imagine that the satisfaction they want will come to them if, in overcoming some difficulties which confront them, they can thereby open the door to repose.

Thus life passes away. Man seeks repose in combating some obstacles; if they are surmounted rest becomes intolerable. For either we dwell in thought on the miseries we have, or on those which are impending. And, even if we saw ourselves sheltered on all sides, *ennui* of its own accord would not fail to arise from the bottom of our hearts, where it has its natural roots, and fill the mind with its venom.

The advice given to Pyrrhus, to accept the repose he tried to find by so much toil, encountered great difficulties.

Thus man is so unhappy that he would be weary, even if no cause of weariness existed, owing to the peculiarities of his disposition; and such is his frivolity that in the presence of a thousand actual causes of uneasiness the merest trifle, such as a game at billiards or at tennis, will divert him.

But, you will say, what is his object in all this? To boast to-morrow among his friends that he has played a better game than any one else. In the same way others toil in their closets to show to men of science that they have solved a problem in algebra hitherto undiscovered; and so many others expose themselves to the greatest perils to boast afterwards of having taken a certain place, quite as foolishly as it seems to me. And finally others shorten their lives in observing all these things not in order to grow wiser thereby, but simply to show that they know them, and these are the most foolish of the band since they are so consciously, while we may

42

suppose with regard to the others that they would not be so foolish if they were better informed.

Some man passes his time without weariness by playing each day for small stakes. Give him every morning the money which he could gain by gambling any day, but on condition that he does not play, and you will only make him unhappy. It may be said, perhaps, what he wants is amusement, not gain. Let him play for nothing, he would not only lose zest but grow weary over it. It is, then, not amusement alone that he seeks; a languid and passionless amusement will weary him. He must get excited over it, even if he must deceive himself into imagining that he would be happy in gaining what he would refuse to accept as a gift on condition that he should not play. He must make himself an object of passion to excite his desire, anger, fear on account of the object in view, as children get frightened at the faces blackened by themselves.

Whence is it that this man, who has lost a son only a few months ago and who, overwhelmed by law suits and wrangling, was so much troubled this morning, has at the present moment forgotten all about it? Be not surprised : his mind is altogether taken up with watching whither the boar will run, pursued by the hounds in hot haste for the last six hours. That is enough. Man,

43

however poignant his distress, if he can be persuaded to give himself up to some diversion, will be happy while it lasts. And, however happy he may be, unless he have his mind diverted, or occupied by some passion or amusement, which prevents *ennui* spreading, he will soon be dispirited and made miserable. Without diversion there will be no joy, with diversion no sadness. And this, too, forms the happiness of persons in high station, it is because they have a number of persons to amuse them, and the power to continue in that state.

Take notice of this, what is it to be superintendent, chancellor, first president, but to be in a position to have a crowd of people coming in the morning from every direction, not leaving an hour in the day for self-reflection? And if they are in disgrace and sent for retirement to their country-houses, where they are in no want of means and servants to minister to their needs, this does not prevent their being miserable and desolate, because here is no one to hinder them from thinking about themselves.

Is not the royal dignity in itself great enough for the possessor to render him happy merely by the contemplation of it? Must he, too, be diverted from this thought like ordinary beings? I can well conceive that a man can be rendered happy by diverting attention from the sight of his domestic sorrows by being absorbed entirely in

44

the effort to dance well. But is it the same in the case of a king, and will he be more happy by attending to frivolous amusements than by the contemplation of his own grandeur? What more satisfactory object could be presented to his mind? Would it not interfere with his joy to occupy his mind by adjusting his steps to the cadence of an air, or skilfully throwing a bar, instead of giving himself up to the restful contemplation of the majestic glory by which he is surrounded? Try the experiment and leave the king to himself, without any gratification of the senses, without any anxiety of mind, without society, with full leisure for self-reflection, and you will find that a king without diversion is a man full of misery. Also people take good care to avoid this, they always place a considerable number of people round the person of a king, who are on the watch so that amusements follow the business of state, and who take care that all his leisure hours are furnished with pleasures and games so as to leave no gap, that is to say kings are surrounded by persons, who take uncommonly good care so as to protect the king from self-reflection, knowing that he would be miserable, though he is a king, if he thought about himself.

I do not speak at all here of Christian kings, as Christians, but only as kings.

The only thing that consoles us in our miseries is diversion and is in itself the greatest of all our miseries. For it is the main hindrance preventing us from thinking about ourselves and leads insensibly to our destruction, without it we should feel weary, and this feeling of weariness would compel us to seek a more solid means to escape from it. But diversion amuses us and brings us to the grave by imperceptible advances.

Men, not being able to find a remedy for death, misery, ignorance, have taken counsel to banish thought about these in order to secure their own happiness.

Nature, making us unhappy in all conditions of life, our desires picture to ourselves a happy state by adding to our state the happiness of the state in which we are not; and even if we could attain to these pleasures we should not be happy, for in that case we should have other desires conformable to this new state.

Imagine a number of men in chains, all condemned to death, some of whom are executed daily in sight of the rest; then those who are left see their own fate in that of their fellows, and regarding each other with sorrow and without hope, wait till their turn comes: this is a picture of man's condition.

B. MAN AND SOCIETY.

Opinions and Customs.

The people honour persons of good birth, the half-informed despise them, averring that birth is not a matter of personal superiority, but of accident. The really intelligent honour them, not for popular, but for deeper reasons. Devotees, who have more zeal than knowledge, despise them in spite of the consideration which makes the latter respect them : for they judge by a new light, which their piety gives them. But mature Christians honour them by another and superior light. So there is a succession of opinions for and against, according to the amount of light given us.

We have shown, then, that man is frivolous by the esteem he bestows on things unessential. And all such opinions are proved worthless. We have shown, also, that all these opinions are perfectly sound and that in this way all frivolities being well established, the people are not so frivolous as they are represented. And thus we have invalidated the opinion which destroyed that of the people. Yet we must destroy this last

47

proposition and show the truth is incontestable, that the people are foolish yet their opinions are sound, because they do not feel the truth where it is, and putting it where it is not, these opinions are always very false and very unsound.

It is true, then, to say that all are under an illusion: for though the opinions of the people are sound, this is not the outcome of their thought, for they think that truth exists when it does not. Truth is in their opinions, but not in the direction where they suppose it to be. For example, it is true that noblemen should be treated with consideration, but not because good birth is an effective advantage, &c. The greatest of evils is civil war. These are sure to break out if you try to recompense merit, for all will say that they deserve it. The harm we may expect from a fool, who succeeded by right of birth, is neither so great, nor so certain.

Why do we follow the majority? Is it because they have more reason? No, but because they have more power. Why do we follow ancient laws and opinions? Is it because they are more sound? No, but they are unique and take away the root of diversity.

The empire founded on opinion and imagination lasts for a time and is pleasant and voluntary, that of force is perpetual. So, too, opinion may be the Queen of the world, but force is its tyrant.

We do well to distinguish people by external condition rather than by internal qualities! Which of us shall pass on first, or yield place to the other? The least able? But I am as clever as he is; we have to fight it out. He has four lackeys, and I have only one; that is plain, we have but to count. It is my place to yield and I must be a fool to contest the point. This is a way of keeping the peace, which is the greatest of blessings.

The habit of seeing kings accompanied by guards, drums, officers, and everything which has the mechanical effect of inspiring respect and terror, causes their countenances, when occasionally seen alone, to impress their subjects with respect and fear, because it is not easy to separate in thought their persons from the surroundings with which they are generally associated. And the world, not knowing that this is the effect of habit, thinks it to be the result of inherent force. Hence the expression: The stamp of divinity is imprinted on his face, &c.

The power of kings is founded on the reason and the folly of the people, more frequently on their folly. The greatest and most important thing in the world is founded on weakness, and the foundation is admirably firm; for nothing can be more certain than that the people will be feeble. What is founded on sound reason is ill-founded, as the estimate of wisdom.

St Augustine saw that we labour with an uncertain aim on the sea, in battle, &c., he saw not the doctrine of chances which proves that we must do so. Montaigne saw that we are irritated by a halting mind and that habit is all-powerful, though he failed to see the reason of that effect. All these men saw the effects, but did not see the causes. In relation to those who have discovered the causes, they are as those who have only eyes in regard to those who have only intellect; for the effects may be perceived by the senses, while the causes are only visible to the intellect. And although these effects may be seen by the intellect, this intellect is to the mind, which sees causes, as the bodily senses are to the intellect.

How is it that a lame man does not offend us, yet a halting mind does offend us? Because the lame man allows that we walk straight, but the halting mind says that it is we who limp; were it not for this, we should pity him rather than be angry with him.

Epictetus asks with greater force how it is that we are not amazed if any one tells us that we have a headache, but are annoyed when we are told that we reason badly, or make a bad choice? The reason of this is, that we are quite sure that we have no headache (and that we are not lame), but we are not so sure that we make the proper choice. The only assurance we have of this is that we see with our whole power of sight whilst another sees the opposite with the whole power of his sight; this puts us into a state of suspense and surprise; and, still more so, if a thousand others ridicule our choice; for we have to prefer our own light to that of so many others, and this is painful and difficult. There is never any such contradiction in the senses with regard to the lame in body.

Deference consists in the readiness to put ourselves to inconvenience. This may seem absurd, but it is really just, for it means that I would put myself out readily if I could serve you, since I do it willingly, though it can be of no service to you. Besides, deference serves to distinguish people of rank. If respect consisted in sitting in an armchair, we should pay respect to everybody, and so there would be no distinction; but where it is done with inconvenience to ourselves the distinction is obvious.

The people have very sound opinions: for example: in the first place, they prefer amusement and the chase to poetry. The half-cultured ridicule this, and point to it triumphantly, as an instance of the world's folly; yet, for a reason they fail to fathom, the people are right. Secondly, they distinguish men by externals such as wealth and good birth: the world, again, exults in pointing out the unreasonableness of this; yet it is quite reasonable. (Savages laugh at an infant king.) Thirdly, they are offended by a blow, or desire glory overmuch. Yet the latter is very desirable on account of real advantages attached to it. And a man who has received a blow without resenting it will be overwhelmed with indignities and straits. Fourthly, they are working for an uncertain aim, going to sea, or walking over a plank.

There is a great advantage in high birth, it puts a man forward at an age of eighteen to receive consideration and respect, which another could only secure by merit in the course of fifty years! This is a gain of thirty years without trouble.

Have you never seen people, who, in complaining of the small notice you have taken of them, parade before you the example of people in position, who have an esteem for them? I would answer them in this way: "Show me the merits whereby you have charmed these persons, and I will esteem you in the same way."

ESTEEM RESTS ON BORROWED QUALITIES

If a man place himself at a window to watch the passers-by, suppose I am one of these, can I assert that he sits there to see me? No; for he does not think of me in particular. But he, who loves a person for her beauty, does he really love her? No, for the smallpox, without ending fatally, may destroy her beauty and cause love to cease. And if any one loves me for my judgment, or my memory, does he love me? No, for I might lose these qualities without ceasing to exist. What, then, is this *me*, if it consists neither in the body nor in the mind? And how can you love body or soul save for those qualities, which are not the *me*, since they are perishable? For could any one love the substance of a person's mind in the abstract with some inherent qualities? that is impossible and would be unjust. Hence we can never love a person, but only his qualities. Therefore let us not hold up to ridicule those who claim honour on account of rank or office, for no one is loved except on account of borrowed qualities.

Things which have most hold on us, such as concealment of the smallness of our means, frequently amount to next to nothing. It is a mere nothing, magnified into a mountain by our imagination. Another turn of the imagination leads us to expose them readily enough.

Few possess the power of invention; the greater majority are willing to follow and refuse the glory of inventors, who try to get it by their discoveries. If they persist in their claim and despise those who are not inventors, these will give them nicknames, if not blows. Let them not pique themselves upon such acuteness, or else be content to be themselves.

Justice, Law, Social Ethics.

The world contains all the good maxims, nothing more is required, but their application. For example, we are bound without doubt to expose our lives for the defence of the public good, and several do it, but not for religion.

Inequality, then, must be among men, that is true; but thus much being granted, this opens a door not only to the greatest domination, but also the greatest tyranny. There must be some kind of relaxation to the mind. But this opens the door to the greatest excesses. Some limit must be marked out. There are no limits in the things themselves, laws try to lay them down, but the mind cannot bear them. Reason often is more imperious in her demands than a master: for in disobeying the one we are unhappy, and in disobeying the other we are fools.

54

JUSTICE THE OUTCOME OF CUSTOM

Why do you kill me? Why? Do you not live on the other side of the river? My friend, if you lived on this side, I should be an assassin, it would be unjust to kill you in this way; but since you live on the other side, I am a brave man, I am doing the right thing. Those who live without rule charge those who live by law that they are deviating from nature and that they themselves follow nature, just as people in a vessel think that those on the shore recede from them. The use of language is the same everywhere. We must have a fixed point to judge on the matter. The harbour decides for those on the vessel, but where shall we find a harbour in morality? As fashion makes what is agreeable, so it makes what is justice.

Justice is that which is established; and thus all established laws will necessarily be held as just without further examination because they are established.

The only universal rules are the laws of the country in ordinary things, and the majority rule in other cases. Whence is this? From the power they possess.

For this reason kings, who have the power in other respects, do not follow the majority of their ministers.

Without doubt equality of goods is just; but,

not being able to enforce obedience to justice, they make justice to consist in obedience to force; not being able to fortify justice, they justify force so that justice and force may unite and peace ensue, which is the sovereign good.

Summum jus, summa injuria. The majority is the best way because it is visible and has the power to compel obedience; yet it is the opinion of the least able.

If it had been possible they would have put power into the hands of justice; but as force cannot be controlled at will, being a material quality, whereas justice is a spiritual quality, which is at the disposal of will, they have handed it over to force, and so they call that, which has to be observed by compulsion, justice.

Hence the right of the sword; for the sword gives a true right (otherwise we should see violence on one side and justice on the other). To this we must ascribe the violence of the Fronde, which raises its pretended justice against force. It is not so in the Church, for here there is true justice and no violence.

It is right that what is just should be obeyed, it is of necessity that what is strongest should be obeyed. Justice without force is powerless: force without justice is tyrannical. Justice without force meets with opposition, for there will be always the wicked. Force without justice is arraigned. Hence the necessity of bringing justice and force together, making what is just strong and what is strong just.

Justice is subject to dispute; force is easily recognised and beyond dispute. Thus we cannot give force to justice, because it is opposed to justice, calling it injustice, averring its own justice: and so, not being able to make that what is just strong they have made that which was strong just.

When it becomes a question whether we ought to make war and kill so many human beings, condemn so many Spaniards to death, it is one man alone, who is the judge and he is an interested party. There should be a third and disinterested person.

Such speeches as the following are tyrannical: I am beautiful, therefore I ought to be feared. I am strong, therefore I ought to be loved. Tyranny is the wish to have in one way what can only be had in another. Diverse duties are owing to diverse merits: the duty of love to the amiable; of fear to the powerful; the duty of assent to those who have knowledge. These duties should be rendered; we have no right to refuse, nor is it right to require others. It is equally erroneous and tyrannical to say: He has no power, therefore

I shall pay no regard to him: he is not clever, therefore I shall not fear him.

There are some vices which have only a hold on us through others, and these, like branches, fall with the removal of the trunk. When malice has reason on its side, it becomes proud and displays reason in all its splendour: when austerity, or a rigid choice, has not found the true good, and it is found necessary to return to nature, it becomes proud of this return.

If man were happy, he would be so all the more, being less amused like the saints of God.

Yes, but does not happiness consist in being able to find pleasure in amusement? No, for it comes from elsewhere and from without: and so is independent of, and from the outset is subject to, being troubled by a thousand accidents, which make afflictions inevitable.

Extremes, whether in excess or defect of reason, are accused of madness. Nothing but mediocrity is good. The majority has settled this, and carps at any one who escapes from it in any direction. I will not object to this, I am quite willing to be placed there, and refuse to be at the lower end, not because it is low, but because it is at the extremity. For the same reason I would refuse to be placed at the upper end. To leave the mean is to leave humanity; the greatness of the human mind is to know how to keep there. So far from greatness consisting in leaving it, it rather consists in not leaving it.

Man is full of wants, he only loves those who can satisfy them all. He is a good mathematician, say they. But I have nothing to do with mathematics, he would take me for a proposition. He is a good soldier. He will take me for a besieged place. What is wanted is a gentleman, who can adapt himself to all my wants in a general way.

We should not be able to say either that he is a mathematician, a preacher, or an orator; but that he is a gentleman. This quality of universality is the only one that pleases me. It is a bad sign when on seeing a man you call to mind his book. I could wish that no other quality were noticed than that which meets the case to make use of it. *Ne quid nimis*, for fear lest one quality master the man so as to be designated by that. We should not think of such an one as a good speaker except it be a question about oratory, but think of it only in that case.

When in health we wonder what we should do if we were sick; but when sickness comes we take medicine cheerfully, into this the evil resolves itself. We have no longer those passions and desires after amusements and exercises, resulting

59

from a state of health, but which are incompatible with the exigencies of our complaint. Nature supplies the passions and desires suitable to the present state of things. Nothing troubles us but apprehensions which we, not nature, create for ourselves; because they join to our present condition the passions and the condition in which we are not.

Discourses on humility furnish material for pride to vainglorious persons, and humility to the humble. So, those about scepticism become matter of affirmation to believers. Few talk humbly of humility, chastily of chastity, few of scepticism doubtingly. We are nothing but falsehood, duplicity, contrariety, we hide and disguise ourselves from ourselves.

Noble actions are most estimable when they are concealed. When I discover some of them in history they afford me great delight. But after all they have not been quite concealed since they have come to be known; and though people have done all they could to hide them, the little outlet, by which they become known, spoils all, since the most beautiful part of all was the wish to hide them.

Maker of Epigrams, a Bad Character.

Self is hateful. You, Miton, conceal it, but do not get rid of it. Hence you do not cease to be hateful. — Not at all, for in acting as we do, obliging everybody, there is no cause for their hating us. — That is true, if we only hated in the *self* the uneasiness it causes us. But if I hate it because it is unjust in making itself the centre of everything, I shall always hate it. In a word *self* has two qualities. It is unjust in itself because it makes itself the centre of everything, it is inconvenient to others in trying to make them its slaves. Each *ego* is the enemy and would be the tyrant of all the rest: you remove the inconvenience, but not the injustice; and, therefore, you cannot render it loveable to those who hate injustice: you only render it loveable to the unjust, who no longer find in it their enemy: and so you remain unjust and can only please those who are so likewise.

I do not admire the excess of a virtue, such as valour, unless I see at the same time an excess of the opposite virtue, as in Epaminondas, who possessed extreme valour with extreme benignity, for otherwise it is not to rise, but to fall. We do not exhibit greatness by being at one extremity, but touching both extremities at once and filling up all that lies between the two. But, perhaps, it is only a sudden movement of the soul from one to the other extreme, and that, in fact, it is ever at one point, like a firebrand. Be it so, but this, at least, is a sign of mental agility, if not of large-mindedness.

A little thing consoles us, because a little thing afflicts us.

I had passed much of my time in the study of abstract sciences; and the little opportunity it offered to share it with others gave me a distaste for it. When I began the study of man I saw that these abstract sciences are not his proper study and that I was becoming more estranged from my condition in investigating than others in ignoring it; I forgave them their scanty knowledge. But I thought to find, at least, many companions in the study of man and that this really is his proper study. I was deceived. There are still fewer engaged in this than in the study of geometry. It is only for want of knowing how to study man that we engage in others. But is it not a fact that man is not in need of this knowledge of himself, but to be ignorant of it if he wants to be happy?

When all moves at the same rate, nothing appears to move, as in the case of a vessel, where all tend to excess, none appears to do so. He, who stops, draws attention to the irregularities of the others like a fixed point.

Why should I attempt to divide my morality into four parts rather than into six? Why found virtue on four, two, or one? Why should it consist in *abstine* and *sustine* rather than in "follow nature"? Or, in conducting private affairs without injustice, according to Plato, or any other thing? But you will reply: Thereby you may comprise the whole matter in a word. Yes, but that is useless, unless it be explained; and, if you try to explain it from the moment I make plain the precept, containing all the rest, from this the same confusion arises which at first you tried to avoid. Thus if they are all contained in one they are useless, as in a chest, and only appear in their natural confusion. Nature has established them all without including one in the other.

Nature has made all these truths independent of each other. Our act makes one dependent on the other, but this is not natural. Each has its own place.

If you want to reprove with effect, and to convince another that he is mistaken, you must take note on what side he views the matter, for on this side it is generally true, to admit this truth, and to show him the side where it is false. He will be satisfied with that, for he sees that he was not mistaken; and that, perhaps, arises from the fact that naturally man cannot see everything and that naturally he cannot err on the side open to his view, as the perceptions of the senses are always true.

The strength of a man's virtue should not be measured by his special efforts, but by his ordinary course of action.

The great and the little are subject to the same accidents, the same vexations, the same passions, but the former are near to the circumference of the wheel, the latter near the centre, therefore less agitated by the same revolutions.

Although people may not have any interest in what they say, we must not entirely conclude from that, that they are not lying; for some there are who lie simply for the sake of lying.

The example of Alexander's chastity has not made continent as many as that of his drunkenness made intemperate. It is not a shame not to be as virtuous as he, and seems excusable not to be more vicious than he. We do not consider ourselves to be altogether on the ordinary level of human vice when we find ourselves vicious along with the great; without reflecting that in this particular they are like ordinary men. We hold on to them at the point when they hold on to the people; for however highly they are placed, in this they are conjoined with the lowest in some way. They are not suspended in the air, altogether apart from our society.

No, no; if they are greater than we it is because they hold their heads higher; but their feet are as low down as ours. All are on the same level, and rest on the ground; and in their lower extremities are as low as we are, as the meanest, as children and brutes.

What we like is the combat, not the victory. We like to watch the combat of animals, not the infuriated victor over the vanquished. We only wanted to see the victorious end, and, as soon as it comes, we are cloyed by it. So it is in play, and the same in the search after truth. What we like in disputes is the clash of opinions, but not at all the contemplation of the truth when discovered. To observe it with pleasure it has to be shown as arising out of strife. In the same way as to the passions, there is pleasure in seeing two of them in the shock of opposition; but if one prevails, it becomes mere brutality. We never seek things for themselves, but for the search of things. So on the stage, quiet scenes, suggesting no fears, are worthless, so are extreme and hopeless miseries, brutal lust, excessive cruelty.

We do not teach men to be gentlemen, though we teach all the rest; yet they are never so much piqued for not knowing the rest as they pique themselves on being gentlemen: the only thing they are proud of is that which they have not learned.

To speak of those, who have treated on the

K.   65   5

subject of self-knowledge, the divisions of Charron, which sadden and weary us, the confusions of Montaigne that he was sensible of this want of right method, that he avoided it by skipping from subject to subject and tried to be fashionable! How absurd the attempt of describing himself! and this not in a casual way and in opposition to his maxims, in the way in which most people err; but according to his own maxims, according to his main and principal design! For it is an ordinary failing to say silly things by chance and weakness, but to say them intentionally, this is intolerable; to say such as these....

To pity the unfortunate is not contrary to our propensities; on the contrary, we are quite willing to have to render this proof of friendship and to acquire a reputation for tenderness without giving anything.

Things have different qualities, and the mind has different inclinations; for nothing is simple as presented to the mind, and the mind never gives itself up simply to any given subject. Hence it is that we weep and laugh over the same thing.

Tyranny consists in the desire of rule outside its sphere. There is room for the strong, the beautiful, the sensible, the pious where each man rules at home, not elsewhere. But sometimes they meet; the strong and the beautiful in their folly contend for the mastery, for their supremacy is of different kinds. They do not understand each other and their fault is that they want to rule everywhere. Nothing can bring this about, not even force: it is of no avail in the kingdom of the wise, being mistress only in external actions.

Ferox gens, nullam esse vitam sine armis rati. Some would prefer death to peace: others prefer death to war. Every opinion may be preferable to life, the love of which seems so strong and so natural.

How difficult it is to propose anything for the consideration of another without warping his judgment in the manner of propounding it! If you say, "I think it is fine, I think it is obscure," or anything like it, you influence the imagination into forming the same judgment, or irritate it into a contrary direction. It is better to say nothing; in that case the other will judge according to what really is, and according as the other circumstances have placed it, not of our creation; then, at least, we shall have placed nothing in the way; unless our very silence produce some effect, according to the turn, or interpretation, which the other may be in the humor of giving it, or according to his conjectures, formed from gestures, or the expression of face, the tone of our voice, if he is a physiognomist; so difficult it is not to displace a judgment from its natural place, or rather so little firmness or stability is there in it!

Montaigne is wrong. Custom should only be followed, because it is custom and not because it is reasonable, or just; but the people follow it for the simple reason that they think it is just : otherwise they would not follow it, though it is the custom; for no one is willing to be subject to anything but reason and justice. Custom, then, would become tyranny. But the reign of reason and justice is no more tyrannical than that of desire : these are principles natural to man.

It would be well, then, to obey laws and customs, because they are laws, but it should be understood that there is neither truth, nor justice, to introduce into them, that we know nothing about these and, therefore, follow only what is recognised. Thus we should never transgress them. But people are not susceptible to this doctrine; and, therefore, as they think that truth may be discovered and that it is contained in the laws and customs, they believe these laws and take their antiquity as a proof of their truth and not only of their authority apart from truth. Thus they yield obedience; but are apt to revolt as soon as it is shown that they are worthless, which can be proved in the case of all of them in certain aspects.

The knowledge of external things will not console me for my ignorance of morality in times of affliction; but the science of Ethics will always console me for the ignorance of external knowledge.

Time heals our griefs and dissensions, because of the change we undergo, and are no longer the same person. Neither the offender, nor the offended, remains the same person. It is like a nation whom we have provoked, and meet again, after two generations. They are still the French, but not the same individuals.

Man's Condition: Inconstancy, Weariness, Disquietude.

If any one would have a full knowledge of human vanity he has but to consider the causes and effects of love. Its cause is a "something I do not know what" (Corneille), and the effects of it are terrible. This "I do not know what," so insignificant a thing as to be unrecognisable, disturbs the whole earth, princes, armies, all the world.

Cleopatra's nose: had it been shorter, the whole face of the earth would have been changed.

Caesar was too old, it seems to me, to go for his amusement to conquer the world. The amusement may have suited Augustus, or Alexander : they were young men, whom it is hard to restrain; but Caesar should have been more mature.

The consciousness of the falseness of present pleasures and the ignorance of the vanity of absent pleasures are the cause of inconstancy.

Prolonged eloquence proves tedious.

Kings and other rulers play at times. They do not always sit on their thrones; this would weary them. Grandeur needs to be put off for a time in order that it may be enjoyed. Continuity in all things proves distasteful. Cold is pleasant, to enjoy heat.

Lustravit lampade terras. The weather and my humor have little in common. I have my foggy and fine days within me. Success and failure of my business make little difference : sometimes I fight against fortune; and the glory of the attempt makes it pleasurable, if at times I am disgusted in the midst of luck.

In the act of writing down my thought, it occasionally escapes me; but this reminds me of my weakness which I constantly forget. This is as instructive to me as my forgotten thoughts, for my aim is only to know my nothingness.

It is curious to observe that there are people in the world, who, having renounced all laws of God and nature, have made laws for themselves which they strictly obey, as *e.g.* the soldiers of Mahomed, thieves, heretics, &c. And so, the logicians. It would seem as though their license must be without limit or barriers since they have freed themselves of those that are so just and holy.

"It is my dog," said these poor children.

"This is my place in the sunshine." Here is the origin of the image of universal usurpation.

"You are ungrateful, please excuse my saying so." But for this excuse I would not have known there was anything amiss.—"Reverently be it spoken."—The only evil is their excuse.

We think of Plato and Aristotle in grand robes of pedants. They were worthy people like the rest, having a laugh with their friends ; and when they were amusing themselves in propounding their laws and politics they did so as in play. This formed the least philosophical and serious part of their lives. The most philosophical was to live simply and quietly.

If they wrote in politics, it was as if putting down rules for a lunatic asylum. And when they pretended to speak of it as something grand, they knew that the fools to whom they were talking thought they were kings and emperors. They entered into their principles in order to make their madness as little harmful as possible.

Martial's Epigrams—Men delight in malice,

but not as against the one-eyed and the unfortunate, but against the fortunate and proud : people are mistaken in thinking otherwise. For desire is the origin of all our endeavours, and humanity, &c. We ought to please those who have human and tender feelings.

The epigram about the two one-eyed people is worthless, for it cannot console them and only gives point to the author's glory. All that is merely for the sake of the author is worthless ambition—*Ambitiosa recidet ornamenta.*

A true friend is so great an advantage even for the greatest lords in order that he may speak ever of them, and stand up for them in their absence even ; so that they should try to have one. But they should choose well, for if they spend all their efforts in the interest of fools it will be of no use to them though they speak so well of them, if they happen to be weak, for in that case they lack authority ; and thus they will speak ill about them in company.

Do you want people to speak well of you ? Do not speak of it.

I lay it down as a fact that if all men knew what others say of them there would not be four friends in the world. This is manifest from the quarrels caused by indiscreet reports made from time to time. Death is easier to bear without the thought of it than is the thought of death without peril.

Strange that a thing so palpable as the vanity of the world should be known so little, so that it is a strange and surprising thing to say that it is folly to seek for greatness, this is wonderful !

He, who does not see the vanity of the world, must be very vain himself. And who does not see it excepting young people who themselves are in the turmoil, the diversion, and the thought of the future? But take away their diversion and you will see them dried up with weariness ; they then feel their own nothingness without knowing it. For this is, indeed, to be unhappy to suffer intolerable sadness as soon as we are forced to self-reflection without any diversion.

Everything here is true in part, and false in part. Real truth is not so: it is altogether pure and true. This mixture debases and destroys it. Nothing is unadulterated truth ; and thus nothing is true if by it we understand pure truth. It may be said that it is true that homicide is bad. Yes, for we know well what is evil and false. But who will say what is good? Chastity? But I say: No, for that would mean the end of the world. Marriage? No; for continence is better. Not to kill? No, for there would be terrible disorders, since the wicked could kill all the good.

73

To kill? No, for that would destroy nature. We possess truth and goodness only in part and mixed up with what is false and evil.

Evil is easy, its forms are infinite ; good is almost unique. Yet a certain kind of evil is as difficult to find as what is called good ; often, and for this reason, we allow this particular evil to pass for good.

It requires even an extraordinary greatness of soul to attain to it as well as to the good.

The cords which bind the respect of men for each other are generally ties of necessity : for there needs must be different grades, all men having a desire to rule, but not all being able to do so, whilst some are.

Let us, therefore, imagine them from the beginning in process of formation. Undoubtedly they will contend with each other until the strongest oppresses the weakest, and so, at length, there is a dominant party. But once this is determined, then the masters, who do not wish that the contest should go on, command that the power in their hand should be transmitted as they please. Some place it in the election of the people, others in hereditary succession. Here imagination begins to play its part. Until, then, power compels the fact, force, now resting on the power of imagination in a certain party, in

France in the nobility, in Switzerland in the commons, &c.

These cords, then, binding the respect of men to such and such an individual, are those of imagination.

Since duchies and kingdoms and magistracies are real and necessary, as force rules everything, they are to be found everywhere at all times. But since it is caprice which makes such or such an one ruler, the rule is not constant, and may vary, &c.

We are so unhappy that we cannot take pleasure in anything except on condition of being troubled if it do not succeed, which may happen in a thousand cases, and does happen constantly. He, who could find the secret of rejoicing in good without being troubled by its contrary evil, would have hit the mark. It is like the perpetual movement.

Instinct, Intelligence, Style.

In proportion to a man's intelligence he will be able to discover a greater number of original characters. Ordinary men cannot discover any difference among human beings.

Diverse kinds of sound sense; some in a given order of things, and not in any other where

75

they get astray. Some can readily deduce consequences from a few principles, and this is sound sense, others draw readily consequences in those things where there are many principles. Thus *e.g.* the former have a clear perception of the properties of water, where the principles are few, but the consequences are so nice that it requires an extremely accurate mind to enter into them. And these may for all that not be great mathematicians, because mathematics embrace a great number of principles, and the nature of the mind may be such that it can penetrate easily only a few principles to their depths and least of all those subjects which contain many principles.

There are, then, two classes of mind : one able to penetrate keenly and profoundly the consequences following from principles, and this is the quality of a sound understanding, the other able to understand a great number of principles without confounding them, and this is the mathematical mind. The one is force and exactness of mind, the other breadth of intellect. The one may exist without the other, the mind can be strong and narrow, and, also, comprehensive and weak.

*　　*　　*　　*　　*　　*

All our reasoning reduces itself into yielding to feeling. But fancy is both similar and contrary

76

to feeling, so that it is impossible to distinguish between these opposites. One says my feeling is fancy, the other that his fancy is feeling. There should be a rule. Reason offers herself, but is pliable in every direction, and so there is no rule.

Those who judge of a work by rule are, as regards others, like those who have a watch in respect to others. One says it is two hours ago, the other says it is three-quarters of an hour ago. I look at my watch and I say to one, "You are wearied out," and to the other, "Time passes quickly with you, it is an hour and a half ago," and I laugh at those, who say that time goes slowly with me and that I judge according to my fancy : they do not know that I judge by my watch.

There are many who speak well, but write badly. The place and the audience warm them and draw from their minds more than they would find in them without this warmth.

What food there is in Montaigne cannot be acquired without difficulty, what is faulty (I mean apart from his morals) might have been corrected in a moment if he could have been told that he was too fond of telling stories and talking about himself.

It is trying to form the exception to the rule. It is even necessary to be strict in opposition to this exception. Nevertheless, since it is certain that there are exceptions to every rule, it is important that our judgments of them should be strict, but also just.

Let no one say that I have said nothing new, the arrangement of materials is new. If we play tennis we both play with the same ball, but one of us puts it into a different position. I shall be equally pleased to be told that I have employed words in common use. And, as by a different arrangement the same thoughts do not form different discourses ; so, too, the same words, differently arranged, do not form different thoughts.

We are more easily persuaded, as a rule, by reasons of our own discovery than by those which have come into the minds of others.

It is natural for the mind to believe and the will to love, so that in the absence of real objects, they attach themselves to such as are false. Those great efforts which the soul sometimes assays are things on which it takes no permanent hold. It simply makes a leap at them, not as upon a throne for ever, but only for an instant.

Man is neither angel nor brute, and, unfortunately, he who would act the angel acts the brute.

By knowing any one's dominant passion we can make sure of pleasing him ; yet everybody has his own fancies opposed to his real good, even in the very idea he forms of that good; a singularity which is very disconcerting.

Brutes do not admire each other. A horse does not admire its companion. Not that there is no rivalry between them in the race, but nothing follows from it; for, once in the stable, the heaviest and least shapely does not yield its oats to the other, as men expect to be treated. Their virtue is self-sufficing.

As the mind gets spoiled, so do the emotions. It is by social intercourse that they are inspired. If this be good or bad, it will make or mar them. Hence the importance to know what choice to make in order to improve and not deteriorate in them. And we cannot make this choice unless we have already formed and not spoiled them. Thus we reason here in a circle, and those are fortunate who escape it.

When we do not know the truth of anything it is well that there should be a common error, which determines the human mind, for example, that to the moon is attributed the change of the seasons, the progress of disease, &c. For the chief malady of man is the restless curiosity about things beyond his comprehension; and it is not so bad for him to be in error as to be curious without purpose.

79

The manner in which Epictetus, Montaigne, and Salomon de Tultie wrote is the most in use, that which is most insinuating and which lingers longest in the memory, the most readily quoted, because it wholly consists of thought arising out of the ordinary intercourse of life. As when we speak of the common error that the moon is the cause of everything, we never fail to say that Salomon de Tultie says that when we know not the truth of anything, it is well that there should be a common error, &c., which is the above thought.

The heart has its own order and so has the intellect, which is according to the first principles and demonstration ; not so the heart. We do not prove that we ought to be loved, propounding in order the causes of love : this would be absurd.

Jesus Christ, St Paul, employ the order of charity, not that of intellect, for their aim is intensity, not instruction. So, too, St Augustine. This order consists principally by digression from point to point, which has its bearing to the final aim, to keep it always in sight.

To put a mask on nature, and to disguise her. No more king, pope, bishop ; but *august monarch*, &c.; no more Paris : *Capital of the Kingdom*. There are some places where we must call Paris

Paris, and others where we must say Capital of the Kingdom.

If words are repeated in a discourse, we try to correct them, but find them so appropriate that to alter would be to spoil; we must leave them standing, that is the proper test; and it is the desire to alter which is blind in not perceiving that such repetition is not wrong in this place; for there is no general rule.

Those who force words for the sake of antithesis resemble people who make false windows for the sake of symmetry. Their rule is not to speak correctly, but to fashion correct figures of speech.

There is a certain pattern of charm and beauty which consists in a certain relation between our nature, feeble or strong as the case may be, and the thing which pleases us. Everything formed on this pattern gives us pleasure, be it a house, song, speech, poetry, prose, woman, birds, rivers, trees, rooms, dress, &c. Anything not according to this pattern displeases those who have good taste. And as there is a perfect relation between a song and a house which are made on a good pattern because they are like this unique pattern, though each after its kind; so, too, there is a perfect relation between things made on a bad pattern. Not because the bad pattern is unique, for there are an infinite number of these. But every bad sonnet, for example, whatever the bad pattern on which it is constructed, resembles perfectly a woman dressed according to this pattern. Nothing helps us to understand better the absurdity of a false sonnet than to consider the nature and the pattern on which it is constructed, and then to imagine a woman, or a house, constructed on the same pattern.

When a natural discourse describes a passion, or an effect, we find in our own mind the truth to which we listen, though we were before ignorant of its existence, so that we are inclined to love the person who makes us feel it, since he has apprised us not of what was his, but our possession; and thus this benefit renders him loveable to us quite apart from the fact that this community of thought between us inclines the heart naturally to love him. We want what is pleasant and real, but what is thus agreeable must be taken from truth.

If we see the natural style we feel surprised and delighted; for we expected to see an author and found a man, whereas those who have good taste in examining a book are surprised to find an author where they thought to find a man : *Plus poetice quam humane locutus est.* Those who have a regard for nature show that she can discuss everything, even theology.

The last thing one finds out in writing a new work is to know what to put first in it. We should not turn the mind from one thing to another except for the sake of relieving it, suitable to the time, not otherwise ; for he that relaxes out of season wearies us and he who wearies us out of season makes us languid and we turn away altogether. So much does our perverse concupiscence like to do everything contrary to what those try to obtain from us, who do so without giving us pleasure, the coin for which we will give all that is required of us.

What a vain thing the art of painting is, which attracts our admiration on account of the resemblance of the things we do not admire in the original!

The same sense varies according to the words which express it. The meaning receives its dignity from the words instead of conferring it on them. We must look for examples.

Those who are accustomed to judge by feeling do not understand anything by process of reasoning; for they try at once to enter into it with a single glance and are not in the habit of looking for reasons. Others, on the contrary, accustomed to reasoning according to principles do not understand matters of feeling, looking for principles, and not being able to see things at a glance.

True eloquence makes little of eloquence, true morality makes little of morality ; that is to say, the morality of the judgment makes little of the morality of the intellect, which has no rules. For perception belongs to judgment as science belongs to the intellect, quick perception appertains to the judgment, mathematics to the intellect ; to make little of philosophy is to be philosophical.

All the false beauties for which we blame Cicero have their admirers and in great number. There are many persons who listen to a sermon as they listen to vespers.

Rivers are roads on the march and carry us where we want to go.

Two faces resembling one another make you laugh by reason of their resemblance, though each by itself is not subject to ridicule.

There are those who have true principles, but make a wrong use of them. But the abuse of truths should be punished as much as the introduction of falsehood.

Scepticism. Man a Monster of Contradictions.

The main strength of sceptics, omitting those of lesser importance, consists in this : that we have no certitude whatever concerning truth of first principles apart from faith and revelation, save so far as we have a natural perception of them within ourselves; but this natural perception is not a convincing proof of their truth, since, having no certainty whatever apart from faith whether man is created by a good God, or an evil demon, or by chance, it is open to doubt whether these implanted principles are true, or false, or uncertain according to our origin. Moreover no one has any certainty, apart from belief, whether he is awake, or asleep, considering that in sleep we are firmly persuaded that we are awake; we believe that we see space, figures, and motion; we feel the lapse of time and measure it, and, in short, we act as if we were awake. So that half of our life being spent in sleep, we have, by our own admission, no idea of the truth, whatever we may suppose. Since, then, all our sentiments are illusions, who knows whether the one half of our life in which we think we are awake is not another sleep, little differing from the former, from which we awake when we think we are asleep? I confine myself to the only strong argument of the dogmatics, namely that speaking sincerely and in good faith we cannot doubt concerning natural principles.

In answer to which the sceptics put in one word the uncertainty of our origin, which includes that of our nature; this the dogmatics have been trying to answer ever since the world began. Here there is open war among men in which each must take part and either side with dogmatism, or scepticism; for he who would remain neutral is sceptic above all things. This neutrality is in the essence of factiousness: he, who is not against them, is for them in the most efficient manner; in this appears their advantage. They are not for themselves; they are neutral, indifferent in suspense as regards everything, themselves not forming an exception.

What is man to do in this state? Shall he doubt everything? Shall he doubt whether he be awake, whether he gets pinched, or burned? Shall he doubt whether he is in doubt? Shall he doubt his own existence? We cannot go so far and set it down as a fact that there ever was a real, thorough sceptic. Nature comes to the assistance of imperfect reason and interferes with its wandering to this point.

Will he assert, on the contrary, that he certainly possesses the truth, he, who, if pressed ever so little, can show no title and is forced to let go his hold?

What chimaera, then, is man! what novelty, what monster, what chaos, what a contradiction, what prodigy!—judge of all things, imbecile worm

86

of the dust, depository of the truth, sink of uncertainty and error, the glory and refuse of the universe.

Who shall unravel such a tangle? Nature confounds the sceptics, and reason confounds the dogmatics. What will become of you, then, O man! in your search after your real condition by natural reason? You cannot escape one or the other of these sects, or subsist in any.

Know, then, proud one, what a paradox you are in yourself, humble yourself, imperfect reason; be silent, imbecile nature, learn that man is altogether incomprehensible to man for ever, and learn from your maker your true condition of which you are ignorant, hear God!

For, in fine, if man had never been corrupt, he would in his innocence enjoy both truth and happiness with assurance. And if man had never been other than corrupt he would have no idea of either verity or blessedness. But unhappy as we are, and more so if there were not some grandeur in our condition, we have an idea of happiness and cannot attain to it; we have a conception of an image of truth, and only are in possession of falsehood: incapable of absolute ignorance and certain knowledge, thus much is manifest, that we were once in some degree of perfection from which we have unhappily fallen.

Yet how astonishing is the fact, that the mystery most removed from our knowledge, that of transmission of sin, should be a thing without which we could not have any knowledge of ourselves! For, undoubtedly, nothing so much shocks our reason than the assertion that the transgression of the first man rendered those guilty, who, being so far removed from the source, seem to be incapable of participating in it. This transmission not only appears to us simply impossible, but even most unjust: for what is there more opposed to the rules of our miserable justice than to damn eternally an infant incapable of will for a sin in which it appears to have taken part so little since it was committed six thousand years before it came into existence? Certainly nothing offends us more rudely than this doctrine; and, yet, without this mystery, the most incomprehensible of all, we are incomprehensible to ourselves. The knotty point in our condition takes turns and twists in this abyss, so that man is more inconceivable to understand without this mystery than the mystery itself is inconceivable to man.

All men try to be happy, to this there is no exception. Much as they differ in the means they employ, all tend to the same end. What makes some go to war, and others to stay away,

arises from the same desire in both, attended
with different views. Will never deviates in the
least degree from this object. It is the motive
of all actions in all human beings, even those
who hang themselves.

And yet, after so many years, no one ever
arrived without faith at this point all aim at
continually. All complain, princes and subjects;
nobles and commons; old and young; strong
and feeble; wise and ignorant; sick and sound
of all countries, of all times, in all ages, and in
all conditions.

A trial, so long, so constant and so uniform
should, indeed, convince us of our inability to
arrive at happiness by our own efforts; but the
example affords us little instruction. Similarity
is never so complete but that there is some slight
difference and hence we expect that hope will
not be deceived this time as before. And thus
the present never satisfying us, hope cheats us,
and from one misfortune to another leads us
on to death, the final consummation.

What, then, is the cry, which this desire and
impotence proclaim to us? Is it not that formerly
man possessed true happiness, of which nothing
remains to him now but the mark and empty
trace which he tries in vain to fill up by all
which surrounds him, seeking from things absent

the help he cannot obtain from those present, which are all inadequate? therefore this infinite gulf can only be filled by an infinite and immutable object, that is by God himself. Himself is his true good, and since man has left him, it is a strange thing that there is nothing in nature which has been able to take his place; the stars, the sky, earth, the elements, plants, cabbages, leeks, animals, insects, calves, serpents, fever, pests, wars, famine, vices, adultery, incest. And since he has lost the true good, everything can appear to him as such, even his own destruction, though so contrary to God, as well as to nature and reason.

Some seek good in power, others in research and the pursuit of science, others in the gratification of the senses. Others, who have actually come nearer to the truth, considered it necessary that the universal good, which all desire, should not consist in any of those particular things which can only be in the possession of one, and which, when shared, afflict their possessor more by the want of that which he has not, than they satisfy him by the enjoyment of that which he has. They have learned that the real good must be such that all can possess it at the same time without diminution and without envy, and which none can forfeit against his will.

We are full of matters, which take us out of ourselves.

Our instinct makes us feel that we must seek happiness outside ourselves. Our passions urge us on towards that which is outside ourselves, even when no objects present themselves to excite them. External objects tempt us of their own accord and appeal to us even where we do not think of them. And thus philosophers plead in vain : Retire into yourselves, then you will find your good; we do not believe them, and those who do believe them are the most empty and the most foolish.

They conclude that what we can do sometimes we can do always and that, since the desire for glory produces right action in those whom it dominates, others could do likewise. There are feverish movements which health cannot imitate. Epictetus concluded that since there are consistent Christians, every one can easily be so.

We know truth, not only by the reason, but also by the heart; it is by the latter that we know first principles, and in vain does reasoning, which has nothing to do with these, try to oppose them. Sceptics, who attempt this, do so in vain. We know we are not dreaming, however impotent we may be to prove it by reason; this impotence only proves the feebleness of our reason, not the uncertainty of all our knowledge as they aver. For the knowledge of first principles, as for example, that there are such things at *space, time, movement, numbers*, is as certain as any of those which we owe to reason. And it is on these kinds of knowledge of the heart and instinct that reason rests, and on which all reasoning is founded. The heart feels there are three dimensions in space, and that numbers are infinite; then reason shows that there are no two square numbers of which one is double the other. Principles are felt, propositions inferred; and both with certainty, though by different ways. And it is equally useless and ridiculous for the reason to demand proofs of its first principles from the heart before giving its assent to them, as it would be ridiculous of the heart to demand of the reason a feeling for all the propositions it proves before accepting them.

This impotence would only serve to humiliate reason, which would judge everything, but not to dispute our certainty as if reason alone were capable of instructing us. Would to God that, on the contrary, we never had any need of it, and that we knew everything by instinct and feeling! But nature has refused us this boon;

on the contrary, she has given us very little knowledge of this sort, all the rest can be acquired by reason only.

And that is the reason why those to whom God has given religion by the feeling of the heart are very blessed and quite legitimately persuaded. But to those who have it not, we can only impart it by reason, hoping that that will give it them by the feeling of the heart without which faith would only be human and useless to salvation.

Memory, joy, are only feelings, and even geometrical propositions become so, for reason produces natural feelings, and natural feelings give way to reason.

This eternal warfare between reason and the passions had for its result that those who wished for peace are divided into two sections. The one have attempted to renounce their passions and become gods ; the other wanted to renounce reason and become brutes (Des Barreaux). But neither were able to do so, and still reason remains charging the passions with baseness and injustice and to trouble the repose of those who give themselves up to them ; and the passions keep alive in those who want to renounce them.

We have an incapacity of proof, unsurmountable by all dogmatism. We have an idea of truth invincible against all scepticism.

We long for truth, and find nothing in ourselves but uncertainty. We look for happiness, and find nothing but misery and death. We cannot but desire truth and happiness and are incapable either of certainty or happiness. This desire is left to us as much to punish us as to make us feel from what height we have fallen.

If man is not made for God, how is it that he can be happy in God only? If man is made for God, how is it that he is so opposed to God?

Man does not know in what rank to place himself, he has evidently gone astray and fallen from his true place, without being able to recover it. He seeks for it everywhere with disquiet, in impenetrable darkness, but without success.

Misery being deduced from greatness, and greatness from misery, some have inferred misery in so much that they have taken man's greatness as a proof of it; others have inferred his greatness with all the more force because they have deduced it from misery itself. All that the former could say to prove the greatness has only served as an argument of his misery to the others, because the greater our fall, the more miserable we are, and vice versa, so that the one party carry on the argument against the other in an endless circle: it being certain that in proportion as men are enlightened, they discover both their grandeur and misery. In a word, man knows that he is unhappy; he is unhappy, then, because he is so. Yet he is truly great because he knows it.

If he exalt himself, I humble him; if he abase himself, I exalt him; I always contradict him until he understands that he is an incomprehensible monster.

Contradictions: Man is by nature credulous, incredulous, timid and rash.

PART II.

HAPPINESS OF MAN WITH GOD.

A. Man in Search of Truth.

The Duty of studying Religious Problems; the Venture of Faith.

LET them learn, at least, what that religion is, which they attack, before attacking it. If this religion claimed to have a clear view of God and to possess it openly and unveiled, then, to say that there is nothing in the world demonstrating it with such evidence, would be to attack it. But since, on the contrary, it says that men are in darkness and estranged from God, that he is hid from their knowledge and that this is the very name he gives to himself in the Scriptures—Deus absconditus (Isai. xlv. 15); and, in fine, if it tries at the same time to establish these two things, that God has set unmistakeable marks in the Church whereby to make himself known to those who sincerely seek him, yet concealed in such a way so that he can only become perceptible to

96

those who seek him with all their heart; what can be their advantage when in their professed negligence in their search after truth they complain that there is nothing to prove it to them? For the obscurity, in which they find themselves and on account of which they object to the Church, only serves to establish one of the things it upholds without touching the other, and, far from destroying, establishes her doctrine.

In order to attack it they should urge that they have made every effort to seek it in all directions, and even in matters which the Church offers for their instruction, though ineffectually. If they spoke in this way they would attack one of her claims to truth. But I hope to show here that no reasonable soul exists who can speak in this way; and I even venture to say that no person ever did so. We know very well how those act who are of this turn of mind. They think they have made great efforts to instruct themselves when they have employed a few hours in reading some book on Holy Writ and questioned some ecclesiastic concerning the verities of the faith. After this they boast that they have consulted without success both books and men. But, in truth, I would tell them, as I have often done before, that such negligence is insufferable. It is not here a question of trifling interest of some strange person to treat it in this fashion; but it is a matter which concerns ourselves and our all.

The immortality of the soul is a matter of such great importance to us, it touches us so profoundly, that we must have lost all feeling if we are indifferent as to our knowledge concerning it. All our actions and all our thoughts must take a direction, differing according to whether there are any eternal blessings to hope for, or no, so as to make it impossible to take a step with sense and judgment without regulating it in regard to this point, which ought to be our final aim.

Thus our first interest and first duty is to have a clear view of this subject, on which the whole of our conduct is based. And it is for this reason that among those who are not convinced of it, I make an important difference between those who make every effort to obtain information on it, and those who live on without taking pains, or thinking about it.

I can only pity those who tremble sincerely in this state of doubt, who regard it as the worst of evils, and who, sparing no pains to escape from it, make their inquiry about it their principal and most serious occupation.

As to those who pass their life without

thinking on its final termination, and who, for this simple reason that they find not within themselves light enough to persuade them, neglect to seek it elsewhere and thoroughly to examine whether the opinion is one of those which people receive with credulous simplicity, or of those which, though obscure in themselves, have nevertheless a very solid and indestructible basis,—these I regard in a totally different light.

This negligence in a matter affecting themselves, their eternity, their all, causes in me irritation rather than compassion; it astonishes and overwhelms me: it seems to me monstrous. I do not say this through pious zeal of a spiritual devotion. On the contrary, I think that we should feel in this way from principles of human interest and self-love. And for this we need see no more than what is seen by the least enlightened people.

There is no need of possessing a highly exalted mind to understand that here below there is no true and solid satisfaction; that all our pleasures are vain; that our evils are infinite; and that, finally, death, which threatens us every moment, must inevitably place us in the course of a few years before the terrible necessity of either being destroyed, or rendered miserable for ever.

There is nothing more real or more terrible than this. However brave we try to be, here is the end awaiting the most beautiful life in the world. Let us reflect upon this and then say whether it is not certain that there is no good in this life except in the hope of another existence. That we are happy only in so far as we approach it and that, as there will be no more unhappiness for those who possess a complete assurance of eternity, so there is no happiness for those who have not a glimmer of it.

Surely it is, then, a great evil to be in a state of doubt; but it is an indispensable duty at least to inquire if one is in this doubt; so that he who doubts and does not inquire is altogether very unhappy and unjustifiable. If he is tranquil and satisfied with this and professes so to be and even takes pride in it and makes this condition a subject of joy and self-complacency, I lack the power to describe so extraordinary a creature.

Where are these sentiments derived from? What subject of joy do we find in expecting nothing but misery without mitigation? How can it be a subject of pride to see ourselves surrounded by impenetrable darkness, and how can the following argument occur to a reasonable man?

I do not know who has placed me into this

world, nor what the world is, nor what I, myself, am. I am in a state of terrible ignorance of everything. I do not know what my body is, nor my senses, nor my soul, and that part of myself which thinks what I say, which reflects on everything and on itself, and knows no more about itself than about the rest. I see these dreadful spaces of the universe enclosing me and find myself fixed to a corner of this vast expanse, without knowing why I am put in this place rather than another, nor why this little time given me to live is assigned to this point rather than another of all eternity which went before and shall follow after me. I see nothing but infinities on every side which close round me, as an atom, and as a shadow which endures but an instant and never returns. All I know is that I must soon die; but what I understand the least is death itself from which I cannot escape.

As I know not whence I came, so I know not whither I go; only this I know that whenever I leave the world I sink either into nothingness, or into the hands of an offended God, without knowing which of these two conditions will be my lot in eternity. Such is my state, full of feebleness and uncertainty. And from all this I conclude that I ought to pass all my days without a thought of trying to find out what will happen to me. Perhaps

I might find something to clear up my doubts; but I will not take the trouble, nor take a single step to find out; and after treating with contempt those who will undertake this task, I prefer to go without foresight and without fears to make trial of the great event and allow myself to be conducted gently to death, and in the uncertainty of my future condition throughout eternity.

Who would wish to have for his friend a man arguing after this fashion? Who would choose him among the rest to entrust him with his affairs? And, in fine, what use would such an one serve?

In truth, it is the glory of religion to have for its enemies men that are so unreasonable, and their opposition has so little danger to it that, on the contrary, it serves for the establishment of its truths. For the Christian faith scarcely goes beyond establishing these two things: the corruption of nature and the redemption of Jesus Christ. But I maintain that if they do not serve to show the truth of redemption by the saintliness of their manners they serve at least admirably to demonstrate the corruption of nature by such unnatural sentiments.

Nothing is so important to man as his own state, nothing so formidable as eternity. And for this reason it is unnatural that there should be human beings indifferent to the loss of their being, and the peril of eternal misery. In respect to all other things they are quite different. They are in dread about the least matters, they foresee them, feel them, and the same man who passes so many days and nights in a rage and despair on account of losing a post, or some imaginary insult to his honour, is the very same man who, being aware of having everything to lose at death, is imperturbable, without emotion. It is a monstrous thing to see in the same heart, at the same time, this sensibility for the slightest matters, and this insensibility of the greatest. This is an incomprehensible infatuation, a supernatural supineness which denotes an all powerful force for its cause.

There must be a strange revolution in man's nature to make him glory in this state, in which it seems incredible that any one could be. However, experience has shown me so great a number of them that it would be surprising did we not know that the greater part of those who meddle in this matter dissemble and are not in fact what they seem to be. They are persons who have heard it said that the manners of good society consist in this would-be daring. This is what they call shaking off the yoke, and try to imitate it. But it would not be difficult to make them understand how mistaken they are in thus seeking esteem. This is not the way of securing it, I say, even among men of the world, who judge things sanely, and who know that the only way to succeed is to show ourselves honourable, faithful and of sound judgment, capable of useful service to a friend in a useful way; for men naturally love only what is likely to prove useful to them. But what advantage is it to us to hear a man say that he had finally shaken off the yoke, that he does not believe there is a God to watch over his actions, that he considers himself sole master, only accountable to himself for his conduct? Does he think to induce us by this to have henceforth complete confidence in him, and to look to him for comfort, counsel, and succour in every need of life? Do they pretend to have given as much pleasure by telling us that they hold that our soul is only a little wind and smoke, and, moreover, in a tone of pride and self-sufficiency? Is this a matter to assert gaily? and is it not, on the contrary, a matter to speak of sadly, as the saddest thing in the world? If they thought of it seriously they would see that this is so great a mistake, so contrary to common sense, so opposed to honourable conduct, and so remote in every way from the grand air they try to assume, that they would rather succeed in restoring than corrupting those who might have an inclination to follow them. And, indeed, if you compel them to give an account of their sentiments, and the reason they have for doubting about religion, they will say things so feeble and base as rather to persuade to the contrary. This is what some one said once to one of them. If you go on arguing in this way, he said to them, you will really convert me. And he was right; for who would not be horrified to see himself entertaining sentiments when you have such despicable persons for your companions?

Thus those who feign these sentiments would be very unhappy in restraining their natural bent in order to become the most inconsequent of men. If they feel distressed at the bottom of their hearts because they have insufficient light, let them not dissemble: there is nothing discreditable in this avowal. The only shame is to be shameless. Nothing indicates more an extreme feebleness of mind than not to perceive how great is the unhappiness of man without God; nothing denotes an evil disposition of heart more than not to wish that the eternal promises may be true; nothing is more contemptible than to dare the Deity. Let them, then, leave these impieties to those who are so ill-bred as to be really capable of them; let them, at least, be men of honour if they

cannot be Christians, and let them, in fine, acknowledge that there are only two sorts of people who
can be called reasonable: those who serve God
with all their heart because they know him; and
those who seek him with all their heart because
they do not know him.

But as for those who live without knowing
him, or seeking him, they judge themselves so
little worthy of their own care that they are
unworthy of the care of others; and we must
needs have all the charity for the religion they
despise, not to despise them, so as even to
abandon them to folly. But because this religion
obliges us to regard them so long as they live as
capable of grace which can enlighten them, and
to trust that in a short time they can be replenished
with more faith than ourselves, whilst we can, on
the contrary, fall into the blindness in which they
are, we must do for them what we could wish to be
done for us if we were in their place and to intreat
them to have pity on themselves, and to take, at
least, a few steps if possible to find the light.
If they will bestow a few hours to reading this,
which they spend so uselessly in other things,
whatever be the aversion they bring to it, perchance they may find something; or, in the
worst case, not much. But as for those who
bring to it a perfect sincerity, and a true desire

to discover the truth, I hope they will be satisfied and convinced by the proofs of a religion so divine, which I have here collected, and in which I have followed nearly this order.

Let us judge thus, then, of those who live without thinking of their latter end, who allow themselves to be led by their inclinations and pleasures thoughtlessly and carelessly, just as if they could annihilate eternity by turning their mind away from it, only thinking of making themselves happy for the moment.

Yet this eternity exists, and death, which must open into it, and threatens them every hour, must put them inevitably ere long before the terrible alternative of either being annihilated, or unhappy for ever, without knowing which of these eternities is in store for them. Resting in this ignorance is a monstrous thing, the extravagance and stupidity of which those should be made to feel who pass their lives in it, bringing it before them to confound them by a sight of their folly. For in this way men reason, if they prefer to live in the ignorance of what they are and without seeking enlightenment : I do not know, say they.

Between these two, ourselves and heaven or hell, there is only our life, the most fragile of all things in the world.

A man in a dungeon, not knowing if his death

warrant is made out, having only an hour to learn it in, and that hour enough if he know it is made out, to have it revoked ; it is contrary to nature for him to employ this hour not by informing himself whether the order is given, but by playing a game of piquet. It is in the same way unnatural that men...&c. It is the heavy weight of God's hand.

Thus not only the zeal of those who seek him, is proof of his existence, but the blindness of those who seek him not.

We run thoughtlessly into the precipice after having placed something in front of us to prevent our seeing it.

Errors of the philosophers who failed to discuss the immortality of the soul. The error of this dilemma in Montaigne.

Difficulty of demonstrating the Existence of God by the Light of Nature.

Our soul is cast into the body where she finds number, time, dimension ; on these she reasons and speaks of them as nature, necessity, and cannot believe anything beyond these.

We know there is an infinite, but are ignorant of its nature. As we know it to be false that numbers are finite, so it is true that there is an infinity in number. But what it is we do not know. It is alike wrong to say that it is even or uneven; for by the addition of one it does not alter its nature, yet one is a number, and every number is odd or even; this is true of all finite numbers. In the same way one may well know that there is a God without being able to know what he is like.

We know, then, the existence and nature of the finite, since like it we have limits and extension. We know the existence of the infinite, but are ignorant of its nature since it has extension like ourselves, but, unlike us, it has no limits.

Yet we know neither the existence nor the nature of God, for he has neither extension nor limits. But by faith we know his existence, whereas in a state of glory we shall know his nature. But I have already shown that it is quite possible to know the existence of a thing without knowing its nature; let us, then, speak according to the light of nature.

If there is a God, he is infinitely incomprehensible, since, having neither parts nor limits, he has no relation to us: we are, therefore, incapable to know either what he is, or if he is. This being so, who would undertake to solve the question? Not we, who bear no relation to him.

Who, then, shall blame the Christians for not being able to give a reason for their faith since it is they who profess a religion for which they cannot give a reason? When producing it before the world they declare it to be foolishness, *stultitiam* (1 Cor. i. 19), and yet you complain that they do not prove it! Were they to prove it they would not keep their word. It is the absence of proof which shows that they are not lacking in sense. Yes! but whilst it excuses those who offer it as such, and relieves them from blame for producing it without reason, it does not excuse those who accept it.

Let us, then, examine this point and say: God is, or he is not. But to which side do we incline? Reason has no power to determine anything about this matter, an infinite chaos separates us. There is a game going on at the end of this infinite distance in which it will be heads or tails. Which will you bet on? According to reason you can do this on one or the other; according to reason you cannot back either.

Then do not accuse of error those who have made a choice; for you know nothing about it.— No, but you say: I will blame them for having made not this choice, but any choice; for he who calls head and he who calls tail are equally at fault, both are wrong, the proper thing is not to wager.

THE WAGER, WEIGHING CHANCES

Yes, but we must wager : it is not optional.
You are embarked in the business, which will you
take? Let us see. Since choose you must, let
us see which interests you the least. You have
two things to lose, the true and the good; and
two things to stake, your reason and your will,
your knowledge and your happiness; and your
nature has two things to avoid, error and misery.
Your reason is none the worse for choosing either,
since of necessity you must choose, this is the
point settled ; but your happiness? Let us weigh
gain against loss and cry heads—that God is.
Consider both cases, if you win, you win all ; if
you lose, you lose nothing. Wager, then, that he
is, without hesitation.—That is admirable, yes, I
must wager, but, may be, I stake too much.—Let
us see. Since there is an equal chance of gain
and loss, if you had only two lives to win against
one, still you might wager. But if there are three
to win, you must play (since play you must), you
would be imprudent, since you are compelled to
play, not to stake your one life to gain three in a
game of equal chances. But there is an eternity
of life and happiness. And, this being so, if
there were an infinity of chances, a single one of
which would be in your favour, you still would be
wise to stake one to gain two, and you would be
acting contrary to good sense, being obliged to

play, if you refused to play one life against three in a play where out of an infinity of chances there is one in your favour if there is an infinity of life infinitely happy to gain. But there is here such an infinity of life of infinite happiness to gain against a finite number of chances of loss, and what you stake is finite. The balance is apportioned. Wherever the infinite exists and there is no infinity of chances of loss against that of gain there is no balancing required, we must risk the whole. Thus, if we are compelled to play, we must give up reason for taking care of life rather than hazarding it for infinite gain, which is as likely to ensue as the loss of nothingness (annihilation).

For it is of no use saying that the gain is uncertain, whereas the risk is certain ; and that the infinite distance between the *certitude* of our risk equals, and the *incertitude* of our gain equals, the finite good we certainly risk for the uncertain infinite. That is not so : every player risks the certain to gain the uncertain, yet, nevertheless, he risks the certain finite to gain the uncertain infinite without sinning against reason. There is no infinitude of distance between this certainty which we risk and the uncertainty of gain ; that is untrue. There is in reality an infinity between the certainty of gain and the certitude of loss.

But the incertitude of gain is in proportion to the certainty of risk according to the proportion of chances of loss and gain, and thence it follows that, if the chances on both sides are equal, the step taken is to play on equal terms, and then the certainty of that, which is exposed to risk, is equal to the uncertainty of the gain, so far is it from being infinitely distant. Therefore our proposal has infinite force where it is a question of hazards, the finite in a game where the chances of loss and gain are equal with an infinity of gain. This is matter of demonstration. And if men are capable of any truth, this is one of them.

I confess, I admit it, still there is no means of seeing the hands at the game? Yes, Scripture, and the rest, &c.

Yes; but my hands are tied, and my mouth is closed. I am compelled to wager, and am not free: there is no escape for me and I am made of such stuff that I cannot believe. What, then, do you want me to do?

That is true. But learn at least your own incapacity to believe. Since reason lands you there, and yet you are unable; try your best, then, not to be convinced by an increase of the proofs of God, but by a diminution of your passions. You want to go in search of faith, but do not know the way; you want to be cured of infidelity and you ask for a remedy: learn from those who were bound like you, and who yet wager all their good; they are the people, who know the way, whom you want to follow, and be healed of an evil of which you want to be cured. Follow the way in which they began, that is acting as if they believed, in taking consecrated water, having mass said, &c. Naturally this in itself will make you believe, and you will become simple (1 Cor. iii. 19)....But that is what I am afraid of.—But why? what have you got to lose?

But to show you that this leads there, that it is this that will allay your passions, which offer the greatest obstacle, &c.

And what harm can come to you in taking this side? You will be faithful, honest, humble, grateful, beneficent, sincere as a friend, and true. True, you will not have those poisoned pleasures, glory and luxury, but will you not have others?

I tell you you will gain in this life, and that at every step you make on this road you will see so much certainty of gain, and so much nothingness in what you stake, that you will know at last that you have wagered on a thing which is certain, infinite, and for which you have given nothing in return. O! your words transport me, ravish me, &c.

YOU MUST MAKE A BEGINNING

If my words please you and seem sound, know that they proceed from a man who has thrown himself on his knees before and after to ask the Being infinite and without parts, to whom he commits his all, that you also may submit to him yours for your own good and for his glory, and that this strength may accord with this weakness.

One joined to infinity adds nothing to it, no more than a foot adds anything to an infinite measure. The finite becomes nothing in the presence of the infinite and becomes simply nothing. So it is with our spirit in the divine presence; so with regard to our justice before divine justice. The disproportion between our justice and divine justice is not so great as that between one and infinity. It needs but that the justice of God should be immense like his compassion: but justice towards the reprobate is not so great and should shock us less than his compassion towards the elect.

I should have given up my pleasures at once, they say, if I had faith. And I tell you: you would soon have faith if you had abandoned your pleasures. It is you who must make a beginning. If I could, I would give you faith. I cannot do this, and therefore cannot test the truth of what you say. But you can easily abandon your pleasures and test the truth of what I say.

The metaphysical proofs of God are so remote from human reasoning and so complicated that they strike the mind with little force, and if they are of use, this is only for an instant at which the proof is seen, but an hour afterwards they are afraid of having been deceived.

Quod curiositate cognoverint superbia amiserunt.

Such is the outcome of the knowledge of God which is not derived from Jesus Christ, it is communion with God without a mediator, with the God whom they have known without a mediator. Instead of which, those who have known God through a mediator are aware of their own misery.

(Jesus Christ is the aim of all, and the centre to which all things tend. He who knows him knows the reason of all things.)

Those who go astray do so because they fail to see one of these two things. One may well know God without knowing one's misery, or one's misery without God ; but one cannot know Jesus Christ without knowing both together, God and one's misery.

And for this reason I shall not undertake here to prove the existence of God, or the Trinity, or the immortality of the soul, or anything of this kind by natural reasons ; not only because I do not feel myself strong enough to discover proofs in nature with which to convince hardened atheists, but also because this knowledge, without Jesus Christ, is useless and barren. If a man should be persuaded that the proportions of numbers are immaterial, eternal truths, depending on a primary truth in whom they subsist and which we call God, I should not consider him far advanced towards his salvation.

It is a remarkable fact that no canonical author has ever made use of nature to prove the existence of God. All try to make us believe in him. David, Solomon, &c., never said: The void does not exist, therefore there is a God. It must be that they were more skilful than the most skilled who have appeared since then and made use of it. This is very noteworthy.

It is a sign of weakness to prove God by nature; do not, then, despise the Scriptures on this account; but it is a sign of strength to have known these contradictions, honour the Scriptures on this account.

For let there be no misunderstanding, we are as much automatic as we are intellectual, hence it is not by demonstration that persuasion is effected. How few things there are demonstrated! Proofs can only convince the intellect; the strongest, and best believed proofs are those

of custom : it inclines the automaton, which draws
the unreflecting intellect after it. Who has demonstrated that there will be another day to-
morrow, or that we shall die? Yet is there
anything more readily believed? It is, then,
custom which persuades us of these things, and
it is custom which makes so many Christians,
and which makes Turks, pagans, employments,
soldiers, &c. So, then, we must have recourse to
it, when once the intellect has perceived the truth,
so as to soak and steep ourselves in this belief,
which at all times escapes us, for it is too much
to have always the truth before us. We must
acquire a more easy faith, that of habit, which
without violence, without art, without argument,
makes us believe things and inclines all our powers
to this belief, so that our intellect falls naturally
into it. It is not enough to believe by force of
conviction, when the automaton is inclined to
believe the contrary. Both parts of us must
believe : the intellect by reasons which it is
enough to have seen once in our life ; and the
automaton by custom and by not letting it incline
in the contrary direction. *Inclina cor meum,
Deus* (Ps. cxix. 36).

Faith differs from proof; the one is human,
the other is the gift of God. "The just shall
live by faith." It is this faith which God himself

puts into our heart of which proof is often the instrument; faith comes by hearing, but this faith is in the heart, and makes us say: Not *scio*, but *credo*.

The Notes of true Religion.

True religion should have for its characteristic the obligation of loving God. This is very just. And yet none except our own has enjoined it. Moreover it should have the knowledge of lust and weakness. Ours has it. It ought to have applied the remedies for these; one is prayer. None other has asked of God to love and follow him.

The true nature of man, his true good, true virtue and true religion are things the knowledge of which is inseparable.

In order to establish the truth of a religion it is necessary that it should understand our nature. It must have known its grandeur and littleness and the cause of both. Which has known it except the Christian religion?

Other religions such as the pagan are more popular, for they exist in externals; but they are not for educated people. A purely intellectual religion would be better suited to the educated, but it would be of no use to the people. The Christian religion alone is adapted to all, being composed of externals and internals, it raises the people to the internal, it abases the proud to the external, it is not complete without the two ; for the people must understand the spirit in the letter and the educated must submit their spirit to the letter.

Externals must be added to internals to obtain anything from God, that is, we must put ourselves on our knees, pray with the lips, &c., so that the proud man who was not willing to submit himself to God should now be subject to the creature. To expect help from this external is superstition ; not to be willing to join it to the exterior is being proud.

No other religion has recognised that man is the most excellent of creatures. Some who have best known the reality of his excellence have ascribed the low estimate men form of their nature to meanness and ingratitude ; whilst others, well aware how real is this baseness, have treated with a lofty scorn those sentiments of greatness, which are equally natural to man.

Lift up your eyes to God, say some, look on him whose image you are, who has made you to worship him. You can become like him ; wisdom will bring about this similarity if you will follow it. (Raise your head, freemen, says Epictetus.) Others say to him: Cast down your eyes upon the earth, wretched worms that you are, and look on the beasts, whose companions you are.

What, then, is to become of man? Will he become equal to God, or the beasts? What a terrible chasm! What shall become of us, then? Who sees not in all this that man has gone astray, that he has fallen from his place, that he seeks it with disquietude, that he cannot regain it? And who will direct him? the greatest of men have failed in this.

If there were but one religion, God, indeed, would be manifest. So, too, if there were no martyrs except in our religion.... God being hidden, every religion which does not say that he is hidden is not the true religion, and every religion which does not give a reason for it fails in giving instruction. Ours does all this: *Vere tu es Deus absconditus.*

There would be too much obscurity if there were not some visible marks of truth. That is a marvellous one, that it has been always preserved in a Church, a visible assembly. The clearness would be too great if there were but one opinion in this Church; but in order to recognise what is the true is only to see which is the one that has always existed; for it is certain that the truth has always existed, and that nothing false has always existed.

Belief in a Messiah then has always existed. The tradition of Adam was still fresh in the time of Noah and Moses. Afterwards the prophets predicted him along with other things, which from time to time were coming to pass in the sight of man, proving the truth of their mission and consequently that of their promises touching the Messiah. Jesus Christ worked miracles as did also his apostles, who converted all the heathen; and so all prophecies having been accomplished the Messiah is proved for all time.

When I see man's blindness and wretchedness, when I regard the silent universe and man without light, left to himself, lost, so to speak, in this corner of the universe, not knowing who has placed him there, what he has come to do here, what will become of him when he dies, incapable of all knowledge, I become terrified like a man who should be carried in his sleep into a dreadful desert island, and who should awake not knowing where he is and without the means to escape from it. Thereupon I wonder how people in such a wretched condition do not fall into despair. I see others about me of like nature, I ask them if they are better informed than I am. They tell me that they are not: and thereupon these wretched wanderers, having looked round them, and having seen pleasing objects, have attached themselves to them. As for me, I could not attach myself to them, and considering how strongly it appears that there is something else than what I see, I thought to discover whether this God has not left some mark of himself.

I see several opposing forms of religion and consequently all false except one. Each claims to be believed on its own authority and threatens unbelievers. Yet I do not, therefore, believe them; any one can say this, each can call himself a prophet. But I see the Christian religion fulfilling prophecy, and this is what every one cannot do.

That religion alone which is contrary to nature, contrary to common sense, opposed to pleasure, has been at all times the true religion.

The whole course of things ought to have for its object the establishment and grandeur of religion, men ought to have in themselves sentiments in conformity to its teaching; and, in fine, it ought to be so much the object and centre towards which all things tend, that whoever shall know its principles should be able to give a reason both of the whole nature of man in particular and, also, of the whole course of the world in general.

They blaspheme that which they do not understand. The Christian religion consists of two points. It is equally important to men to know them both, and equally dangerous to ignore either. And it is equally of God's mercy that he has given marks of both. Yet they take occasion to conclude that one of these points does not exist from that which should make them infer the other. Those sages who have affirmed that there is a God have been persecuted, the Jews have been hated, the Christians still more so. They saw by the light of nature that if there be a true religion on earth, the course of all things should tend towards it as its centre. And on this ground they take occasion to blaspheme the Christian religion because they misunderstand it. They imagine that it simply consists of adoration of God, conceived as great, powerful, and eternal, which is, properly speaking, Deism, almost as far removed from the Christian religion as atheism, its exact opposite. Thence they conclude that our religion is not true because they do not see that all things concur to the establishment of this point, that God does not manifest himself to man with all the evidence which is possible.

But let them conclude what they like against Deism, they cannot thence conclude anything against the Christian religion, which properly consists in the mystery of a Redeemer, who, uniting in himself the two natures, human and divine, has delivered men from the corruption of sin to reconcile them to God in his divine person.

It teaches, then, men these two truths together, both that there is a God whom all men are capable to know, and the existence of a corrupt nature, which renders them unworthy of it. It is equally important for man to be acquainted with both these points, and it is equally dangerous to man to know God without knowing his own wretchedness, and to know his own wretchedness without knowing the Redeemer, who can cure him of it. The knowledge of one of these will produce either the pride of the philosophers, who have a knowledge of God, but not of their wretchedness; or the despair of atheists, who know their wretchedness without a Redeemer. And thus, as it is equally necessary for man to know these two points, it is equally by the mercy of God to have them made known to us. This the Christian religion has done; this is its nature. Let them examine the order of the universe on this to see whether all things do not tend towards the establishment of the two main points of religion.

We would be very blind if we did not know ourselves to be full of pride, ambition, lust, feebleness, misery and injustice. And, if in knowing this, we had no desire to be delivered from it, what can we say of such men? What else but reverence can we feel for a religion which knows so well the faults of man, and what but a longing for the truth of religion, which contains the promise of such desirable remedies?

Proof: 1°. The Christian religion by its establishment: itself so firmly established, so fully, being so contrary to our nature.—2°. The saintliness, the elevation, and humility of a Christian soul.—3°. The marvels of Holy Scripture.—4°. Jesus Christ.—5°. The Apostles in particular.—6°. Moses and the Prophets in particular.—7°. The Jewish people.—8°. Prophecies.—9°. Perpetuity, no other religion has perpetuity.—10°. The doctrine which has a reason for everything.—11°. The saintliness of this law.—12°. By the course of the world.

It is beyond doubt after this that, considering what is life and what this religion is, we should refuse to act on the inclination to follow it when once it enters our heart, and it is certain that there is no ground for laughing at those who follow it.

HUMAN WEAKNESS, DIVINE REMEDIES

Proofs of Religion in Human Nature.

The greatness and wretchedness of man are so apparent that true religion of necessity should teach us both that there is in man some great principle of grandeur and a great principle of wretchedness. It should, then, furnish a reason for these astonishing contradictions.

To render man happy it must show him that there is a God; that we ought to love him; that our true happiness is in him, and our sole evil separation from him; that it should recognise that we are full of darkness, which hinders us from knowing and loving him; and that thus our duties obliging us to love God, and our evil concupiscence turning us away from him, we are full of injustice. It should give us a reason of this opposition to God and to our own good, it ought to inform us of the remedies for these infirmities, and the means for obtaining these remedies. Let all the religions of the world be examined and see if there be any other than the Christian religion which will be sufficient for this purpose.

Shall it be the philosophers, who propose for the only good, the good in ourselves? Is this the true good? Have they found the remedy for our ills? Is this the way of curing man's presumption by making him equal to God? Have those who have made us equal to the brutes, and the Mahomedans, who have given us earthly pleasures as the sole good even in eternity, produced a remedy for our concupiscence?

What religion, then, will teach us how to cure pride and lust? What kind of religion will teach us what is our good, our duties, the weaknesses turning us aside from these, the cause of these weaknesses, the remedies which can heal them, and the means of obtaining these remedies? All other religions have failed in this. Let us see what the wisdom of God can do! "Do not expect," she says, "either truth, or consolation from men. It is I who have formed you and I only can teach you what you are. But you are not now in the state in which I formed you. I created man holy, innocent, perfect; I filled him with light and intelligence; I communicated to him my glory and my wonders. The eye of man then gazed upon the majesty of God. He was not then in the darkness which blinds him, nor subject to mortality and the miseries which afflict him. But he could not bear so great glory without falling into presumption. He wanted to become his own centre and independent of my aid. He withdrew himself from my rule; and making himself equal to me from a desire to find

happiness in himself, I have left him to himself;
setting in revolt the creatures, which were subject
to him, I made them his enemies, so that man is
now become like the beasts, and so far removed
from me that he scarcely retains a dim light of
his author : so far have all his perceptions become
extinct, or confused ! The senses, independent of
reason and often its masters, have led him away in
pursuit of pleasure. All creatures either torment
or tempt him and domineer over him, either sub-
duing him by their strength, or winning him over
by their allurements, a tyranny more awful and
imperious. Such is the actual state of men.
There remains to them some feeble instinct of
the happiness of their former state, they are
plunged in the misery of their blindness and
sensuality, which have become their second
nature. From these principles I have laid open
to you you may recognise the cause of so many
contradictions which have astonished mankind
and have divided them into so many opinions.
In the meantime observe all the movement of
grandeur and glory, which the conviction of so
many miseries cannot stifle, and see if the cause
of them must not be in another nature.

"It is in vain, O men, to look for the remedies
of your miseries within yourselves. All your light
can only enable you to know that you can never

find in yourselves the truth, or the good. Philosophers have promised it to you, but could not bring it about, they neither know your true good nor your real condition. How could they have provided the remedies for your disorders, which they have not even known? Your principal maladies are pride, which draws you away from God, but which makes you cling to the earth; and they have done naught else than cherish at least one of these maladies. If they have presented God for your object this was only to excite your pride; they have made you think that you are like him and conformable to his nature. And those who have seen the emptiness of this pretension have thrown you on the other precipice in giving you to understand that your nature is equal to that of the beasts, and have induced you to seek your good in lusts which are the portion of brutes. It is not here where the means are to heal you from your disorders, which these sages never knew. I alone can make you understand who you are."

If you are united to God it is by grace, not by nature. If you are abased it is by penitence, not by nature.

The two states being open to you, it is impossible that you should not recognise them. Follow the course of emotion, observe yourself, see if you cannot trace the lively characteristics of these two natures. Can there be so many contradictions in so simple a subject?

"I do not intend that you should believe me without reason, neither do I aim at your subjection by tyranny. I do not aim at giving you a reason for everything and to reconcile these contradictions. I intend to make you see clearly by convincing proofs those divine marks in me, which will assure you who I am, and which will confer on me authority by marvels and proofs which you could not refuse, so that consequently you will believe rationally the things which I teach you when you shall see no further cause for refusal, unless you cannot yourselves know whether they are, or are not."

If there is only one origin of all things there is only one end of all things : all by and for him. Therefore true religion must teach us to love and to adore him only. But since we are unable in ourselves to adore what we do not know, or to love aught but ourselves, the religion which instructs us in these duties must also instruct us in this inability and teach us the remedy for it. She teaches us that by one man all was lost and the bond broken between God and ourselves and that by one man the bond was repaired. We are born so contrary to the love of God and it is so necessary that we must have been born culpable, or else God would be unjust.

Original sin is foolishness in the sight of men, but it is presented as such. Therefore you ought not to reproach me for want of reason in this doctrine as I present it as in its nature without reason. But this foolishness is wiser than all the wisdom of men. "The foolishness of God is wiser than men" (1 Cor. i. 25). For without this how can we say what man is? His whole condition depends on this imperceptible point. And how could it be perceived by his reason since it is a thing contrary to reason, and which reason, far from discovering it in her own way, turns away from when it is offered to her?

This double nature of man is so plain that there are some who have thought that we have two souls: one single subject appeared to them incapable of variations of this knowledge and so sudden from immeasurable presumption to a dreadful abasement of heart.

All these contradictions which appeared to take me further from the knowledge of religion brought me all the more readily to the truth.

Without this divine knowledge what could men do except this: Either to uplift themselves by what remains of the inner consciousness of their past grandeur, or to be cast down in view of their present feebleness? For not seeing the whole truth they could not attain to perfect virtue. Some considering nature as incorrupt, others as incurable, they could not either escape pride or sloth, the two sources of all vice; since they cannot but either abandon themselves through baseness, or escape it through pride. For if they knew the excellency of man they would be ignorant of his corruption; so that they would, indeed, avoid idleness, but only to fall into pride. And if they recognised natural infirmity they would be ignorant of its dignity; so that they would be able, indeed, to avoid its vanity, but this by plunging into despair.

Hence arose the various sects of Stoics and Epicureans, dogmatics and the men of the academy, &c. Christianity alone has been able to cure these two vices, not in expelling one through the other by earthly wisdom, but in expelling both by the simplicity of the Gospel. For it teaches the just in that it elevates them to become partakers of the divine nature, that in this state they still carry about them the source of all corruption, which during their life-time renders them the subjects of error, misery, death and sin; and it proclaims to the most impious that they are capable of the grace of their Redeemer. Thus, making those tremble whom it justifies, and consoling those whom it condemns, religion so justly tempers fear with hope by the twofold capacity common to all of grace and of sin that it humbles infinitely more than reason alone can do, but without despair, and it raises infinitely more than natural pride, but without puffing up: thus making it plain that, being exempt from error and vice, to it alone it appertains to instruct and correct men.

Who, then, can withhold belief and adoration to this heavenly illumination? For is it not as clear as the day that we feel in ourselves ineffaceable marks of excellence? And is it not equally true that we feel at times the effects of our deplorable condition? And does not this chaos and this monstrous confusion proclaim to us but the truth of this twofold state in a voice so powerful that it is impossible to resist it?

Christianity is strange! it requires man to acknowledge that he is vile and even abominable and yet commands him to try to become like God. Without such counterpoise this elevation would render him horribly presumptuous, or this abasement would render him horribly abject.

Misery tends to despair, pride to presumption. The incarnation shows man the grandeur of his misery and the grandeur of the necessary remedy.

The philosophers never recommended sentiments suitable to these two states. They inspired sentiments of pure greatness, which is not man's condition. They inspired sentiments of pure baseness, and that is not man's condition. We must have feelings of abasement not due to nature, but to penitence; not to remain in this state, but to go on to greatness. We must have emotions of greatness not due to merit, but to grace, and after having passed through abasement.

No one is so happy as the true Christian nor so reasonable, virtuous or amiable. With how little pride does the Christian believe in his union with God! With how little abjectness does he put himself to a level with the worms of the dust! What a beautiful manner in accepting life and death, good and evil!

Incomprehensible.—Not all that is incomprehensible is for this reason non-existent. Infinite numbers. Space infinite equal to finite.

It is incredible that God should unite himself to us. This is a consideration drawn from the sight of our vileness. But if this view be accepted sincerely, follow it as far as I do and acknowledge that we are actually so vile as to make ourselves incapable of knowing whether his mercy cannot render us capable of him. For I would know whence this animal, who acknowledges himself so vile, has the right to measure God's mercy and to limit it according to his fancy. He knows so little what God is that he does not even know what himself is : and altogether perplexed by the sight of his own state he dares to say that God cannot render him capable of communion with him! But I would demand of him whether God asks anything else of him but to love in knowing him, and why, since man is by nature capable of love and knowledge, he believes that God cannot make himself known and loved by him. Undoubtedly he knows of his own existence at least and that he loves something. Then if he sees something in the darkness around him and if there be some subject to love among the things on earth, why, if God imparts to him some ray of his essence, should he not be capable of knowing him and loving him in the manner it shall please him to communicate himself to us? There is, then, no doubt, an intolerable presumption in these sorts of arguments, though they seem founded on apparent humility, which is neither sincere, nor reasonable, unless it make us confess that, not knowing of ourselves what we are, we can only learn it from God.

DOUBT, CERTAINTY, SUBMISSION

Submission and Use of Reason.

The last process of reason is to recognise that there is an infinity of things which transcend it. It is only feeble if it does not go so far as to know that, and if natural things transcend it, what shall we say of supernatural?

We ought to know where to doubt, where to feel certain, where to submit. Who fails in this understands not the force of reason. There are those who violate these three rules either in making certain of everything, as demonstrative, for want of knowing what demonstration is; or in doubting everything for want of knowing where we ought to submit; or in submitting for want of knowing when we ought to judge.

Submission and the use of reason, in which true Christianity consists:

If we submit everything to reason, our religion would have nothing mysterious and supernatural. If we violate the principles of reason, our religion would be absurd and ridiculous.

St Augustine. Reason would never submit if she did not judge that there are occasions where she must submit. It is right, then, that she should submit where she judges that she ought to submit.

Piety is different from superstition. To carry

piety as far as superstition is to destroy it.
Heretics reproach us with this superstitious submission. This is to do that with which they reproach us.

It is not an unusual thing to have to reproach the world for too much docility. It is a natural vice like incredulity and as pernicious. Superstition.

There is nothing so conformable to reason as this disavowal of reason.

Two excesses: to exclude reason, to admit nothing but reason.

Faith expresses well what the senses do not express, but not the contrary of what they perceive. It is above them, not contrary to them.

If I had but seen a miracle, they say, I should be converted. How can they be sure that they would do that of which they are ignorant? They imagine that this conversion consists in an adoration which establishes a kind of intercourse and converse with God such as they picture to themselves. True conversion consists in annihilating oneself before this Universal Being whom we have provoked so many times and who might justly destroy us at any time; to recognise that we cannot do anything without him, and that we have deserved nothing from him but displeasure. It consists in knowing that there is an invincible opposition between God and ourselves; and that without a mediator there can be no intercourse. Do not be astonished to see simple people believing without reason. God imparts to them the love of himself, and hatred of themselves. He inclines their heart to believe. People will never believe with practical trust and faith unless God inclines their heart, and they will believe as soon as he does incline them. And this David knew full well. *Inclina cor meum, Deus* [*in testimonia tua*].

Those who believe without having read the testaments do so because they have an inward, altogether holy disposition, and that what they hear said about our religion is in agreement with it. They feel that a God has created them. They only want to love God and to hate themselves only. They feel that they have no power of themselves; that they are unable to go to God; and that, if God does not come to them, they are incapable of any communion with him. And they hear it said in our religion that we must only love God and hate ourselves; but all being corrupt, and unworthy of God, he has made himself man to unite himself to us. There is no need of further persuasion of men, who have such a disposition of the heart and have a knowledge of their duty and their incapacity. Those, whom we see to be Christians without a knowledge of the prophecies and proofs, do judge as correctly as those who have that knowledge. They judge by the heart as the others by the intellect. God himself inclines them to believe and thus they are efficaciously persuaded.

I admit readily that one of these Christians, who believe without proof, will not, perhaps, be able to convince unbelievers, who himself would say as much. But those who know the proofs of religion will prove without difficulty that such a believer is truly inspired of God, though he cannot prove it himself. For God having said in his prophets (who are beyond doubt prophets) that in the kingdom of Jesus Christ he will pour out his Spirit upon the nations, and that the sons, the daughters, and the children of the Church would prophecy, undoubtedly the Spirit of God is upon them and not in the others.

Religious Inquiry and Revelation.

It is absurd to rely on the society of our equals. Unhappy as we are, feeble as we are, they will be of no help to us; we die alone; we should act, then, as though we were alone; and, if so, should we build superb mansions, &c.? We should seek the truth without hesitation; and if we regret it, it is a proof that we value man's esteem more than the search after truth.

This is what I see and what troubles me. I look on all sides and see nothing but obscurity. Nature offers me nothing but matter for doubt and disquiet. Did I see nothing, then, indicating a Divinity, I should decide in favour of denying him. Did I see everywhere the marks of a creator, I should peacefully rest in faith. But seeing too much for denial and too little for assurance, I am in a pitiful condition, and one in which I wished a hundred times that if God sustained nature, she would mark the fact unequivocally; and that if the marks she gives of it are deceptive, she would suppress them at once. Let her say all, or nothing, so that I might see what part I should take. Whereas in my present state, ignorant of what I am or what I ought to do, I neither know my condition nor my duty. My heart entirely inclines me to know where the true good is in order to follow it. Nothing would be to me too dear for Eternity....

I see the Christian religion founded on an earlier religion, and this is what I find of positive fact. I do not speak here of the miracles of Moses, of Jesus Christ and his apostles, because they do not seem at once to be convincing, and I only want to put here in evidence all those grounds of the Christian religion which are beyond doubt and cannot be called into question by any one whatever....

I see, then, plenty of religions in various parts of the world, at all times. But they contain not the morality which pleases me nor the proofs which can arrest me. And thus I should have refused equally the religion of Mahomed and that of China, that of the ancient Romans, and that of the Egyptians, for the sole reason that none have any more the stamp of truth than another, nor anything what of necessity could determine me, reason cannot lean any more on one than another.

But in considering thus this unsettled and strange variety of manners and beliefs of diverse ages, I find in the corner of the world a peculiar people, separated from all other nations of the earth, the most ancient of all, whose records precede by several centuries the most ancient in our possession. I find this people great and numerous, sprung from one man, adoring one God and guiding themselves by a law, which, they say, they received from his hands. They maintain that they are the only people to whom God has revealed his mysteries...that God will not leave for ever the other nations in darkness; that a deliverance will come for all; that they are in the world to announce him to men; that they have been expressly formed to become the fore-runners and heralds of this great event and to call on all nations to join with them in the expectation of this deliverer.

To meet with this people is astonishing and appears to me worthy of attention. I look at the law, which they boast to hold from God, and find it admirable. It is the first law of all and is of such a kind that even before the term *law* came into use among the Greeks it had been received and obeyed uninterruptedly by the Jews nearly a thousand years earlier. In the same way I find it equally strange that the first law in the world happens also to be the most perfect, so that the greatest legislators have borrowed their own from it, as appears from the law of the Twelve Tables thence taken later by the Romans, and as it would be easy to prove, if Josephus and others had not sufficiently treated of the matter. But this law is at the same time the most severe and rigorous of all regarding their religious worship, imposing on this people to keep them to their duty by a thousand peculiar and tedious obser-vances on pain of death. Whence it is a matter of astonishment that it has been constantly ob-served through so many centuries by a people rebellious and impatient like this, while all other states have changed their laws from time to time, although these were much easier to obey. The book which contains this law, the first of all, is itself the most ancient book in the world, those of Homer, Hesiod and others coming into existence six or seven centuries later.

B. MAN IN POSSESSION OF THE TRUTH.

Judaism and Christianity.

In this inquiry the Jewish people draw at once my attention by a number of admirable and singular things to be observed there.

I see to begin with that it is a nation entirely composed of brothers: and whilst all the others are formed by the accumulation of an infinite number of families, this one, though so large, proceeds from one man; and these, being all of one flesh and members one of another, compose a powerful state consisting of one family. This is unique.

This family, or this people, is the most ancient of all known to man; which seems to draw upon them a particular veneration, but principally in our present inquiry; since if God had at all times communicated himself to man, it is to these we must go to ascertain the tradition.

144

This people is not only of importance on account of its antiquity, but it is still more singular by its continued existence, from its origin up to the present day: for whereas the people of Greece and Italy, of Lacedaemon, Athens and Rome and the rest, who came a long time after, have perished long ago, these subsist always; and in spite of so many powerful kings trying a hundred times to put them out of existence, as their historians testify, and as it is easy to imagine according to the actual order of things during such a long spell of years, these nevertheless have been preserved, and, extending from first to last, their history includes in its duration that of all the other histories taken together....

God, willing to show that he could call into existence a holy people of invisible sanctity and to fill it with eternal glory, created things visible, as nature is an image of grace; so that men might judge that he was able to make the invisible inasmuch as he could make so well the visible. Thus he saved this people from the deluge, caused them to be raised up from Abraham, redeemed them from their enemies, and caused them to enter into rest.

Grace itself is the figure of glory, for it is not the ultimate end. It was prefigured by the law, and itself prefigures glory, but it is a figure of it, and its origin, or cause.

The ordinary life of man resembles that of the saints. All seek their satisfaction and differ only in the object wherein they place it. They call those their enemies who hinder them in this, &c. God, then, has shown the power which he has to bestow invisible gifts in that he manifested it in things visible.

God, willing to deprive his own of perishable goods, in order to show that this was not through lack of power, called into existence the Jewish people.

The Jews grew old in these earthly thoughts that God loved their father Abraham, his flesh, and that which would spring from it. That for this reason he had multiplied them and separated them from all other nations, not permitting them to intermingle; that when they languished in Egypt he brought them out with all these great signs in their favour; that he fed them with manna in the desert; that he brought them into a very fat land; that he gave them kings and a temple well built, there to offer beasts, by the shedding of whose blood they might be purified; and that at last he would send the Messiah to make them masters of the whole world; and foretold the time of his advent.

The world having grown old in these carnal errors, Jesus Christ came at the time predicted, but not with the expected splendour; and for this reason they did not believe that it was he. After his death St Paul came to teach men that all these things happened in figures; that the kingdom of God did not consist in the flesh, but in the spirit, that man's enemies are not the Babylonians, but his passions; that God was not pleased with temples made with hands, but with pure and contrite hearts; that circumcision of the flesh is unprofitable, but that of the heart was needed; that Moses had not given them the bread of heaven, &c.

But God, not willing to disclose these things to this people unworthy of them, and yet willing to foretell them in order that they might be believed, predicted the time clearly, and expressed the things sometimes clearly, but very often in figures, so that those, who loved the emblems, might rest in them, and those who loved the things figured might see them therein.

The carnal Jews neither understood the grandeur, nor the abasement of the Messiah as predicted in their prophecies. They misunderstood him in his predicted grandeur, as when it says that the Messiah should be David's lord, though his son, and that he is before Abraham and that he saw him. They did not believe him to be so great as to be eternal: and in the same way misunderstood him in his abasement and in his death. The Messiah abideth for ever, said they, and this man said that he would die. They did not believe in him either as mortal or immortal: they were looking in him for a carnal grandeur.

The Jews loved the shadows so much and waited for them so entirely that they misunderstood the reality and its appearance at the time and in the manner predicted.

Prophecies preceding his coming were necessary to inspire faith in the Messiah and also that they should be conveyed by an unsuspecting people of extraordinary diligence, fidelity and zeal, and known throughout the world. To effect all this, God selected this carnal people, into whose custody he placed the prophecies predicting the Messiah as deliverer and dispenser of carnal goods in which the people took delight; and thus they had an extraordinary ardour for these prophets, having had charge of these books predicting the Messiah before the whole world, assuring all the nations that he had to come, and in the way foretold in these books, which they held open before in the universe. And thus this people, undone by the poor and ignominious

148

advent of the Messiah, became his most cruel enemies. So, then, we have here a people of the world least suspect of favouring our belief, the most exact and zealous that can be named for the law and the prophets so as to hand them down intact. For this reason the prophecies have a hidden meaning, the spiritual, to which this people were opposed, concealed in the carnal to which they were friendly disposed. If the spiritual sense had been revealed, they would not have been able to love it; and, not being able to hear it, they could not have been zealous of the preservation of their books and ceremonies. And if they had loved these spiritual promises and had preserved them intact till the days of the Messiah, their testimony would have had no force because they had been his friends. For this reason it was well that the spiritual sense was hidden. But, on the other hand, if the sense had been hidden in such a way that it could by no means have appeared, it could not have served as proof of the Messiah. What was it, then, that happened? It was hidden under the temporal in a multitude of passages and was so clearly discovered in some; besides the time and state of the world were foretold so plainly that it is clearer than the sun: this spiritual sense is so clearly explained in several places that no less a blindness than that which the flesh imposes on the spirit, when subject to it, can keep us from recognising it.

Such were the dealings of God. This sense is concealed under another in an infinite number of passages and revealed rarely in some, but yet in such a way that the passages where it is concealed are equivocal and can suit both senses, while those passages where it is plain are unequivocal and can only suit the spiritual meaning. *Fac secundum exemplar quod tibi ostensum est in monte* (Exod. xxv. 40). The religion of the Jews was, then, formed to resemble the truth of the Messiah; and the truth of the Messiah has been recognised by means of the Jews' religion, which prefigured it. In the Jews the truth was shadowed forth. In heaven it is revealed. In the Church it is concealed and recognised by its correspondence with the type. The type was founded on truth and the truth was recognised from the type.

He who could judge the religion of the Jews by the carnal ones would judge it badly. It is seen in the sacred writings and in the tradition of the prophets, who have sufficiently explained that they did not understand the law literally. In the same way our religion is divine in the evangelists, the apostles and tradition; but it is absurd in those who treat it badly.

CARNAL JEWS AND CHRISTIANS

The Messiah, according to the carnal Jews, should be a great temporal prince. Jesus Christ, according to carnal Christians, came to free us from the duty of loving God, and to give us sacraments which do everything without us. Neither one or the other is the Christian religion, or the Jewish. The true Jews and the true Christians have at all times expected a Messiah, who should make them love God, and, by this love, to triumph over their enemies.

There are two sorts of men in each religion. Among the heathen worshippers of beasts, and others, again, who are worshippers of one God, in natural religion. Among the Jews, the carnal and the spiritual, who were the Christians of the old law. Among Christians, the coarse ones, who are the Jews of the new law. The carnal Jews look for a carnal Messiah; and the coarse Christians believe that the Messiah has dispensed them from the love of God. The true Jews and true Christians adore a Messiah who makes them love God. The carnal Jews and Pagans have their miseries, and so, too, the Christians. There is no redeemer for the heathen, for they simply expect none. There is no redeemer for the Jews, for they wait in vain for him. There is a redeemer only for the Christians. The veil, which is upon these books of the Jews, is then, also, for the Christians, and those who do not hate themselves. But how well disposed men are to understand them and to know Christ when they truly hate themselves! The carnal Jews occupy midway between Christians and Pagans. The heathen know not God and only love this world. Jews know the true God, and love this world only. Christians know the true God and do not love the world. Jews and Pagans love the same God. Jews and Christians know the same God. The Jews were of two kinds, some only had pagan, others had Christian affections.

Evidently they are a people expressly formed to be the witnesses of the Messiah (Isaiah xliii. 10; xliv. 9). They hear about the books they love, but do not understand them, and all this was foretold that God's judgment might be entrusted to them, but as a sealed book.

For this reason I reject all other religions: for this I find an answer to all objections. It is just that a God so pure should only discover himself to those whose heart is purified. Hence this religion attracts me and I find it sufficiently authorised by so divine a morality; but I find yet more there. I find more effective force in the fact that, as far as human memory reaches, it was constantly announced to men that they are in a state of universal corruption, but that some one should come to remedy this. That it is not one man, who said this, but an infinite number of men and a whole nation, prophesying and expressly made, in the course of four thousand years....Thus I stretch out my arms to my deliverer, who, having been foretold for four thousand years, has come to suffer and die for me on the earth at the time and under the circumstances which had been foretold; and by his grace I await death in peace, in the hope of being eternally united to him. And meanwhile I rejoice to live amid both the good things he is pleased to bestow upon me, and the evils he sends me for my good, and which he has taught me to suffer by his example. The more I examine them, the more I find truth in them; both in what has gone before and what has followed: in fine, these, without idols, or king: and this synagogue, which was foretold, and these wretches who follow its use, and who, being our enemies, are admirable witnesses of the truth of these prophecies in which their miseries and even their blindness are foretold. I find this concatenation, this our religion altogether divine in its authority and its duration, in its perpetuity, its morality, and in its conduct, its doctrine, in its effects: the frightful darkness of the Jews predicted: *Eris*

153

*palpans in meridie, Dabitur liber scienti litteras,
et dicet, Non possum legere* (Isaiah xxiv. 12).

Types and Figures.

There are types clear and demonstrative, and
there are others, which seem far-fetched and
which convince only those who are already persuaded. They are in the nature of apocalyptics.
But there is this difference that the latter are not
beyond doubt. So that there is nothing so unjust
as to pretend that theirs are as well founded as
some of ours; for they have not the same demonstrative force as ours. The two cases are, therefore, not parallel. We must not treat in the same
way and confound these things, for they seem to
agree in one point, while they are different in
another. Clearness in things divine deserves our
reverence for what is obscure.

Jesus Christ was typified by Joseph, the well-
beloved of his father, sent by the father to look
after his brothers, &c., innocent, sold by these for
twenty pieces of silver and thereby becoming their
master, their saviour, the saviour of strangers and
the saviour of the world; which would not have
taken place without their endeavour to kill him,
he being sold and disowned by them.

In prison Joseph, innocent between two

criminals, Jesus Christ on the cross between two thieves. He foretells the deliverance of one of them. From the same omens Jesus Christ saves the elect and condemns the reprobate after the same crimes. Joseph can only foretell, Jesus Christ can make it come to pass. Joseph requested the one whose life would be saved to remember him when he came into his glory. He, whom Christ saves, asks that he would remember him when he came into his kingdom.

The synagogue does not perish because it was figure, but because it was figure only, it fell into servitude. The type continued until the truth came so that the Church should always be invisible either in the presentation, which promised it, or the substance.

To prove both testaments with one stroke we need only to see if the prophecies contained in one are fulfilled in the other. To examine the prophecies we must understand them; for if we think that they have only one meaning it is certain that the Messiah has not come; for if they have two meanings it is certain that he came in the person of Jesus Christ. The whole question, then, is to know whether there are two meanings.

To show that the Old Testament is only figurative and that by temporal possessions the prophets understood others, this, in the first place, would be unworthy of God; in the second, their discourses express very clearly the promise of temporal goods and that they say, nevertheless, that their discourses are obscure and that the sense will not be understood. From which it appears that this hidden meaning was not that which they express openly, and that consequently they knew that they meant to speak of other sacrifices and another deliverer, &c. They say that it would not be understood until the end of time (Jerem. xxx. *ult.*).

The third proof is that their discoveries are contradictory and mutually destructive, so that if it is thought that by the words law and sacrifice they only understood those of Moses, there is a gross and palpable contradiction. Therefore they meant something else, sometimes contradicting themselves in the same chapter....

The cipher has two senses: If we intercept an important letter where we find the meaning is clear and where, nevertheless, it is stated that the meaning is veiled and obscure, that it is hidden, so that we see the letter without seeing it, and understand without understanding it; what are we to think, but that it is a cipher with a double meaning; and all the more if we find there manifest contradictions in the literal sense? How

greatly ought we to esteem those who interpret
the cipher to us, and teach us to know the hidden
meaning; and especially if the principles deduced
are altogether natural and clear! This is what
Jesus Christ did and the apostles. They removed
the seal, he has rent the veil and laid bare the
spirit. For this reason they have taught us that
men's enemies are the passions, that the redeemer
is to be spiritual and his kingdom spiritual, that
there are to be two advents, one of humiliation to abase proud humanity, the other of glory
to exalt the humble man; that Jesus Christ is
God and man. The prophets said clearly that
Israel would always be loved of God and that the
law would be eternal, and that its meaning would
not be understood and that it was veiled.

The letter kills. Everything happened in
figures. This is the cipher St Paul gives us. It
was necessary that Christ should suffer. A God
humiliated. Circumcision of the heart, true
fasting, true sacrifice, a true temple. The prophets have indicated that all this is spiritual.

All that tends not to charity is figurative.
The sole end of Scripture is charity. All that
tends not to that one end is a figure of it; for
since there is but one end, all which does not
make for this in express terms is figurative.

God has so varied this sole precept of charity

to satisfy our curiosity, which seeks for diversity, by that diversity which leads us to what alone is necessary for us. For one thing only is needful, yet we love diversity; and God testifies both by these diversities which lead to the only thing needful.

The Rabbis take the breasts of the spouse for a figure and everything else that does not express their sole object, which was temporal good. And Christians even take the Eucharist as a type of the glory, which is their aim.

There are those who see clearly that man has no other enemy than concupiscence, which turns him away from God, and not God; that there is no other good but God; and not a rich land. Those who believe that the good of man is in the flesh and his evil in that which takes him away from pleasures of the senses, let them satisfy themselves in these and die in them. But as for those who seek God with all their heart, whose only grief is to be deprived of a sight of him, who have no other desire but to possess him, and no other enemies but those who turn them away from him, who are only grieved in seeing themselves surrounded and dominated by such enemies;—let them take comfort, I announce to them good news: for them there is a liberator; I will show them there is a God for them; to the others I will not show him. I will show to them that a liberator has been promised, who would deliver them from their enemies, and that one is come to deliver them from their iniquities, but not from enemies.

All these sacrifices and ceremonies, then, were either figures, or absurdities. But there are things clearly too high for us to consider them as absurdities.

The Greatness of Christ.

The infinite distance between body and mind is a type of the infinitely more infinite distance of mind and charity, for it is supernatural.

All the splendour of greatness has no lustre for those who seek the things of the intellect. Intellectual grandeur is invisible to kings, the wealthy, conquerors, and to all the great ones according to the flesh. The greatness of wisdom, which is nothing, if not of God, is invisible to the carnal and men of mere intellect. These form three orders differing in kind. Great geniuses have their empire, their splendour, their greatness, their conquests, their lustre, and have no need of carnal greatness with which they have nothing to do. They are seen, not by the eye, but by the intellect; that is enough. Saints have their empire, their splendour, their conquests, their victory, their lustre, and have no need of either carnal or spiritual greatness, with which they have nothing to do; for they add nothing to these, neither do they take away. They are seen of God and the angels, not by the bodily eye, nor the curious minds: God is enough for them.

Archimedes without pomp would be held in the same admiration. He has fought no conspicuous battles, but he has furnished all minds with his discoveries. Oh! how he has illuminated the minds of men! Jesus Christ, without riches, without any external production of science, stands in his own order of saintliness. He made no discoveries, he never reigned, but he was humble, patient, holy, a saint of God, a terror to evil spirits, free from all sin. Oh! but with what pomp and a transcendent magnificence did he come, to the eyes of the heart, which see wisdom!

It would have been useless for Archimedes to play the prince in his works on geometry, though he was that. It would have been useless for our Lord Jesus Christ, for the purpose of shining in his reign of holiness, to come as kings come: but he came appropriately in all the glory of his order.

It is absurd to take offence at the lowliness of Jesus Christ, since the humiliation belongs to the same order as the grandeur which he came to exhibit. Let them consider this grandeur in his life, in his passion, in his obscurity and in his death, in the selection of his followers, in their desertion of him, in his secret rising from the dead, and the rest; it will be found so vast that there is no cause for taking offence at an abjectness, which is not found there. But there are those, who can only admire carnal greatness as if there were no intellectual ones; and there are others, who can only admire intellectual ones, as if there were not those infinitely higher in Wisdom: all corporeal things, the firmament, the stars, the earth and its kingdoms are not worth the most insignificant mind; for it knows all this and itself; but bodies know nothing. All the bodies taken together and all the spirits taken together with all they produce are not worth the least movement of charity; this belongs to an infinitely higher order.

From all the bodies taken together we could not educe one little thought: this is impossible and belongs to another order. Of all the bodies and spirits one could not extract a simple motion of true charity; that is impossible and belongs to another, the supernatural order.

...Jesus Christ in an obscurity (as the world speaks of obscurity) that the historians only writing about important state affairs scarcely take notice of him.

What man ever had greater renown? The whole Jewish people foretells him before his coming. The Gentiles adore him after his coming. Both Jews and Gentiles look to him as their centre. Yet what man ever enjoyed less his renown! Out of thirty-three years he passed thirty in retirement. For three years he passes for an impostor; the priests and principal men reject him. His friends and relations despise him. At last he dies betrayed by one of his own and denied by another and abandoned by all.

What part, then, had he in all this renown? Never man had more glory; never man more ignominy. All this renown was for our sakes, to enable us to recognise him, and none of it for himself.

Jesus Christ said noble things so simply that it seems as if he had not thought upon them; yet so tersely that it is easily seen what he thought about them. This clearness joined with simplicity is wonderful.

Who taught the evangelists the qualities of a soul so entirely heroic, to paint it so perfectly in Jesus Christ? How is it they present him weak in his agony? Were they not able to paint constancy in death? Yes, for the same St Luke paints that of St Stephen as more firm than that of Jesus. They represent him, then, as capable of fear before the need of dying came and after it as quite strong. But when they picture him so afflicted, it is when he afflicts himself, and when men afflict him he is quite strong.

The Church had as much difficulty to show that Jesus Christ was man against those who denied it, as she had to show that he was God, and the appearances were as strong against the one as against the other.

Jesus Christ is a God whom we approach without pride and before whom we abase ourselves without despair.

The conversion of the pagans was only reserved for the grace of the Messiah. The Jews were so long opposed to them without success; all that Solomon and the prophets had said proved of no avail. Wise men like Socrates and Plato could not persuade them.

...Jesus Christ to whom both testaments bear reference, the old in its expectation, the new as its model, both as their centre. The prophets predicted, but were not foretold, the saints were foretold, but were not foretellers, Jesus Christ was both foretold and a foreteller.

Jesus Christ for all, Moses for a people...."I

163   11—2

will also give thee a light to the Gentiles, &c."
(Isai. xlix. 6). Thus Jesus Christ is an universal
being. The Church herself only offers sacrifice
for the faithful, Jesus Christ, himself on the Cross
for all.

Prophecies concerning Christ.

The strongest proofs of Christ are the prophecies. For these, therefore, God made the
greatest provision ; for the event which has
fulfilled them is a standing miracle from the
commencement of the Church to the end. God,
too, raised up prophets during sixteen centuries,
and during four hundred years after, the prophecies were dispersed with all the Jews, who
carried them with them in all parts of the world.
Such, then, was the preparation for the birth of
Christ, whose Gospel, exacting belief from all
men, made prophecies necessary not only so as to
induce belief, but so that these prophecies should
be spread all over the world that the whole world
might be induced to embrace it.

If a single man had written a book of predic-
tions about Jesus Christ, as to the time and
manner of it, and Jesus Christ had come according
to his prophecies, this would have had infinite force.
But here we have much more. Here we have a

succession of men during four thousand years, who constantly and without variation come one after another, foretelling the same event. A whole people announces his coming and continues to exist for four thousand years to testify in a body to their certainty, from which they cannot be diverted by all the threatenings and persecutions to which this people are exposed: this is far more important.

Effundam spiritum meum. All the nations had been in unbelief and lust; the whole world was now ablaze with love. Princes leave their grandeur, maidens suffer martyrdom; whence comes this power? It sprang from the advent of Messiah. This was the effect and these were the marks of his coming.

He should teach man the perfect way (Isai. ii. 3), and never has there come, before him, or after, any man who taught anything divine approaching this. Then Jesus Christ comes to tell men that they have no other enemies but themselves, that it is their passions which separate them from God; that he is come to destroy these and to give them his grace, so as to make them a holy Church; that he has come to bring back into this Church both heathen and Jews; that he comes to destroy the idols of the one and the superstitions of the other.

To this all men are opposed, not only from the natural opposition of their lust, but, above all, the kings of the earth join together to destroy the new born religion as it had been foretold. *Quare fremuerunt gentes? Reges terrae adversus Christum.* All that is great on the earth is united together, the learned, the wise, the kings. The first write, the second condemn, the last kill. And notwithstanding all these oppositions, these men weak and simple resist all these powers, subdue even these kings, scholars, and sages, and remove idolatry from all the earth. And all this is done by the power which had foretold it.

Moses, Mahomed and Christ.

It is a remarkable matter and worthy of special attention to see this Jewish people existing during so many years in perpetual misery: it being necessary as a proof of Jesus Christ and that it continues for the sake of this proof, and in misery, because they have crucified him; and, though to be miserable and yet continuing to exist are contradictory, this people continues to exist nevertheless in spite of its misery.

Mahomedanism has for its foundation the Alkoran and Mahomed. But this prophet, who ought to be the last hope of the world, had he been foretold? What mark has he, which may not be equally possessed by any man, who would call himself a prophet? What miracles are there which he affirms to have performed? What mystery has he taught according even to his own tradition? What was the morality and what the happiness offered?

The Jewish religion must be differently regarded in the handing down of the sacred books and in the tradition of the people (and it is the same with all religions, for Christianity in the holy Scriptures is very different from the casuists). Its morality and felicity are ridiculous in the tradition of the people, but it is admirable in that of the saints. Its foundation is wonderful: it is the most ancient book in the world, and the most authentic; and whereas Mahomed, to ensure the lasting existence of his book, forbade men to read, Moses, to secure continuity for his own, has commanded everybody to read it.

Our religion is so divine that any other divine religion is only the foundation of it.

Mahomed, not foretold; Jesus Christ, foretold. Mahomed, killing; Jesus Christ, causing death in his own. Mahomed forbidding to read; the apostles commanding us to read.

Finally, the two are so contrary that if Mahomed took the way to succeed humanly,

Jesus Christ took the way to perish humanly. And in place of concluding that since Mahomed has succeeded Jesus Christ could easily have succeeded, it must be said that since Mahomed has succeeded Jesus Christ ought to have perished.

God seen by some and hidden from others.

God has willed to redeem mankind, and open the way to salvation to those who sought him. But men render themselves so unworthy that it is right for God to refuse to some by reason of their hardness what he accords to others by compassion which is not due. If he wanted to overcome the obstinacy of the most hardened he would have done so by revealing himself so clearly to them, that they could not have doubted about the truth of his existence; as he will manifest himself in the last day, with such a crash of thunderings and so great a convulsion of nature, that the dead will rise and the blind will see.

It is not in this way that he wished to appear in his gentle advent; because so many prove themselves unworthy of his clemency he determined to leave them deprived of the food for which they had no desire. It was not right, therefore, that he should appear in a manner manifestly divine, and absolutely capable of convincing all men, but it was equally unjust that he should come in a way so hidden that he could not be recognised by them who sincerely sought him. He wanted to make himself completely known to these; and thus, willing to appear plainly to those who seek him with all their heart, and concealed from those who flee from him with all their heart, he tempers the knowledge of himself in such a manner as to give signs of himself visible to those who seek him, but not to those who seek him not. There is light enough for those who only want to see, and darkness enough for those of a contrary disposition. There is clearness enough to see for enlightening the elect and obscurity sufficient to humiliate them. There is obscurity enough to blind the reprobates and clearness sufficient to condemn them and to render them inexcusable.

If the world existed to instruct man concerning God, his divinity would beam forth from all parts of it in a way which could not be gainsayed; but since it only exists by Jesus Christ and for Jesus Christ in order to instruct men, concerning both their corruption and their redemption, everything then breaks out in proof of these two truths. What appears then neither indicates

169

total exclusion, nor manifests presence of divinity, but the presence of a God who hides himself: all bear this character.

If God had never discovered himself in any way, this eternal privation would be equivocal and might either be connected with the total absence of divinity, or the unworthiness of man to know him. But occasional and not continual appearance removes this ambiguity. If he appeared once, he is for all time; from which we cannot conclude otherwise but that there is a God and that men are unworthy of him. God prefers to sway the will rather than the intellect. Perfect clearness would serve the intellect, but would harm the will. To humble pride.

If there were no obscurity at all, man would not consider his corrupt state; if there were no light at all, man would despair of a remedy. Thus it is not only just, but useful for us that God should be hidden in part and revealed in part, as it is equally dangerous for man to know God without knowing his own misery, and to know his misery without knowing God.

It is, then, true that everything teaches man his condition, but he must understand this well: for it is not true that everything reveals God, nor is it true that everything conceals God. But it is at the same time true that he hides himself from those who tempt him, and reveals himself to those who seek him, for men are altogether unworthy of God, or capable of God; unworthy by their corruption, capable on account of their original nature.

There is nothing on earth, which does not show either the misery of man, or the mercy of God, either man's impotence without God, or his power with God.

What say the prophets of Jesus Christ? That he will be manifestly God? No: but that he is a God truly hidden; that he will be misunderstood; that people will not think that it was he; that he will be a stone of stumbling at which many would dash themselves, &c. Let no one reproach us, then, with want of clearness, since we make profession of it.

As Jesus Christ remained unknown among men, so truth remains among common opinions without external difference. If the mercy of God is so great that his teaching is salutary even where he hides himself, what great light, then, must we expect when he reveals himself?

We cannot understand anything about the works of God unless we take for our principle that he has willed to blind some and enlighten others.

God, as revealed by Christ.

I wonder at the boldness with which those persons undertake to speak of God in addressing their words to the irreligious. Their first chapter is to prove divinity by the works of nature.

I should not be astonished at their enterprise if they addressed their discourse to believers, for it is certain that those, who have a lively faith in their heart, see that everything in existence is the work of God whom they adore. But for those in whom this light is extinguished and in whom it is intended to kindle it, these, destitute of faith and grace, who seeking with all their light whatever they see in nature to lead them to this knowledge, find only obscurity and darkness: to tell them that they need only look at the smallest things which surround them is sufficient in order to see God unveiled, and give them as sole proof of this great and important subject the course of moon and planets, and to pretend to have exhausted the proof of such an argument, is to give them ground for belief that the proofs of our religion are very feeble, and I see from reason and experience that there is nothing more likely to excite contempt for it.

It is not in this way that the Scripture speaks,

172

which knows better the things that are of God; on the contrary, it tells us that he is a hidden God, and that since the corruption of our nature he has left us in a blindness from which we can only escape by Jesus Christ, and except through him we are deprived from all communication with God: *Nemo novit Patrem, nisi Filius, et cui voluerit Filius revelare.*

This is what the Scripture indicates when it says in so many places that those who seek God find him. It is not a light *like the sun at noonday* as we say. We say not that those who seek the sun at noonday, or water in the sea, shall find them; thus it follows that the proof about God is not of this kind. Also it tells us elsewhere: *Vere tu es Deus absconditus.*

The God of the Christians is not a God simply the author of geometrical truths and of the order of the elements; this is the view of Pagans and Epicureans. He is not only a God who exercises his providence on the life and well-being of men, to grant a happy course of years for those who adore him; such was the portion of the Jews. But the God of Abraham, Isaac and Jacob, the Christians' God, is a God of love and consolation: he is a God who fills the soul and the heart of those who are his own. He is the God who makes them feel their inward wretchedness and

173

his infinite pity, who communicates himself to their inmost soul; who fills it with humility, joy, confidence, love; rendering them incapable of an end other than himself.

The God of Christians is a God who makes the soul feel that he is her only good; that her only rest is in him; her only joy in loving him; and who makes her at the same time abhor those obstacles which withhold her from loving God with all her might. The two hindrances, self-love and lust, are insupportable to him. This God makes her feel that the root of self-love destroys her, and that it is he alone who can heal her.

The knowledge of God without that of our misery engenders pride. The knowledge of our misery without that of God produces despair. The knowledge of Jesus Christ forms the middle way because therein we find both God and our misery.

All those who seek God apart from Jesus Christ, and who stop at nature, either find no light to satisfy them, or end in forming to themselves a means of knowing God and serving him without a mediator: thus they either sink into atheism or deism, two things which the Christian religion almost equally abhors.

We know not God but through Jesus Christ. Without this mediator all communion with God is taken away. By Jesus Christ we know God. All who have pretended to know God and to prove his existence without Jesus Christ had but feeble proofs. But for proof of Jesus Christ we have the prophecies which are solid and palpable proofs. And these prophecies, accomplished and proved true by the event, mark the certainty of these truths, and consequently prove the divinity of Jesus Christ. In him, then, and by him, we know God. Apart from that, and without the Scriptures, without original sin, without a necessary mediator, foretold and come, we could not absolutely prove God nor teach sound doctrine and sound morality. But by Jesus Christ and in Jesus Christ we prove God and teach morality and doctrine. Jesus Christ, then, is the true God of man. But we know at the same time our misery, for this God is none other than he who repairs our misery. Thus we cannot know God but by knowing our sins.

Also those who have known God without knowing their misery have not glorified him, but have glorified themselves. *Quia non cognovit per sapientiam, placuit Deo per stultitiam praedicationis salvos facere.*

We know not God only by Jesus Christ, but we do not know ourselves but by Jesus Christ alone. We do not know life or death but by

Jesus Christ. Apart from Jesus Christ we do not know either what is life, or death, God, or ourselves.

Thus, without the Scripture, which has Jesus Christ alone for its object, we know nothing and only see obscurity and confusion in the nature of God and in our own nature.

Without Jesus Christ man must be steeped in vice and in misery; with Jesus Christ man is freed from vice and misery. In him is all our virtue and all our felicity. Away from him there is only vice, misery, errors, darkness, death, despair.

Without Jesus Christ the world would not exist; for it could only be either destroyed, or a very hell.

Thoughts on Miracles.

Miracles are the test of the doctrine and the doctrine is the test of miracles.

There are false miracles and true. There must be some mark whereby we may know them; otherwise they would be useless. Now they are not useless; on the contrary, they are fundamental. Again the rule which is given us must be such that it does not destroy the proof afforded by true miracles to the truth which is the chief end of miracles.

Moses gave two: that the prediction does not come to pass (Deuter. xviii. 22) and that they do not lead to idolatry (*ib*. xiii. 4), and Jesus one (Mark ix. 39).

If doctrine regulate miracles they are useless for doctrine.   If miracles regulate…

If the miracles are true could we prove every kind of doctrine?   No, this would not follow (*Si angelus*… Gal. i. 8).   Rule.   We must judge of doctrine by the miracles, we must judge of miracles by the doctrine.   All this is true but there is no contradiction here.   For we must distinguish the times.

If there were no false miracles, there would be certainty.   If there were no rule for discrimination, these miracles would be useless and there would be no reason for belief.   Now, humanly speaking, there is for man no other certainty but reason.

Every kind of religion is false, which in its belief does not adore God, as the cause of all things, and which in its moral teaching does not love one only God as the end of all things.

The proofs adduced by Jesus Christ and the apostles from the Scriptures are not conclusive; for all they say is that Moses foretold a prophet should come, but by this they do not prove this was he, that is the whole question.   These passages, then, serve only to show that it is not contrary to Scripture, that there is no opposition, but not that there is accord. Now it suffices so that there be no opposition with miracles.

Jesus Christ says that the Scriptures testify concerning him, but does not show in what way.

Even the prophecies could not prove Jesus Christ in his life-time. For this reason there would not have been any guilt in not believing in him before his death, had not the miracles been sufficient without the doctrine. Now those who would not believe him while still alive were sinners, as he says himself, and without excuse (John xv. 22). Therefore they must have resisted a conclusive proof. Now they had not our proof, but only miracles; these are sufficient, then, when doctrine is not contrary and ought to be believed.

Jesus Christ proved that he was the Messiah, never verifying his doctrine by Scripture and prophecies, but always by miracles. He proves that he remits sins by a miracle.

Nicodemus recognised by these miracles that the doctrine was from God. *Scimus quia venisti a Deo magister; nemo enim potest facere quae tu facis, nisi fuerit Deus cum illo.* He does not judge miracles by the doctrine, but the doctrine by the miracles.

There is a reciprocal obligation between God and man. We may forgive the expression: *quid debui* (Isai. v. 4), "Come, let us reason together" (*ib.* i. 18). God must fulfil his promises.

Men are under obligation to God to receive the religion he sends them. God is under obligation to men not to lead them into error. Now they would be led into error if the workers of miracles declared doctrine, which, on the face of it, did not appear false in the light of common sense, and if a great worker of miracles had not previously warned them against believing them. In the same way if there was a division in the Church and that the Arians, for example, who affirm their doctrine, like that of the Catholics, to be founded on the Scriptures, had wrought miracles whilst the Catholics had not done so, we should have been led into error. For as a man who professes to make known divine mysteries is not worthy of credit on his private authority and it is on this account that irreligious people doubt it; so, too, to a man, who to prove his being in communication with God raises the dead, foretells future events, removes the sea, heals the sick, no one, though irreligious, will fail to submit, and the unbelief of Pharaoh and the Pharisees is the effect of a supernatural hardness of heart. When, therefore, we see the miracle and the doctrine suspected for the same reason, we must see which is the clearest. Jesus Christ was under suspicion.

There is a great difference between tempting and leading into error; God tempts, but does not lead into error. To tempt is to supply the occasions which lay us under no necessity for doing wrong if we love not God. To lead into error is to put man under the necessity of following a falsehood.

John vii. 40 seq. Contentions among the Jews as among Christians in the present day. Some believed in Jesus Christ, others did not believe in him on account of the prophecies, which said that he was to be born in Bethlehem. They should have taken more care to see whether this was not so. For, his miracles being convincing, they should have made sure about those supposed contradictions of his doctrine by Scripture; and the obscurity did not excuse, though it blinded them. So those who refuse to believe miracles in these days on account of a pretended flimsy contradiction are inexcusable.

Miracles are more important than you suppose. They served for the foundation and the continuity of the Church up to Antichrist, up to the end.

God either confounded the false miracles, or foretold them; and in either case he raised himself above what is supernatural in regard to us and has raised ourselves to it.

Miracles are of such force that it was necessary

for God to warn men not to believe in them in opposition to him, however clear it may be that there is a God; without which they would have been capable to disturb (i.e. the inmates of Port Royal).

These nuns, astounded at what is said that they are on the road to perdition, that their confessors lead them to Geneva, that they inspire them with the thought that Jesus Christ is not in the Eucharist, nor at the right hand of God, know that this is false; they offer themselves to God, then, in that state: "*Vide si via iniquitatis est in me*" (Ps. cxxxix. 24). What happened thereupon? This place which is said to be the temple of the devil, God makes his own temple. It is said the children ought to be withdrawn (from their instruction). God heals them there. It is said that here is the arsenal of hell: God makes it a sanctuary of his graces. Finally these are threatened with all the furies and all the vengeance of heaven: and God overwhelms them with favours. Those must have lost their senses who conclude that they are on the way to perdition.

The three marks of religion: perpetuity, good living, miracles.

Both Jews and Christians have been told that they should not always believe the prophets. But nevertheless the Pharisees and Scribes make much ado about his miracles and tried to show that they are false and worked by the devil: for they must needs be convinced if they admitted that they are wrought by God.

In the present day we are not obliged thus to discriminate. Yet it is easy to do so. Those who neither deny God nor Jesus Christ work no miracles of an uncertain character: *Nemo faciat virtutem in nomine meo, et cito potest de me male loqui* (Mark ix. 39). But there is no need of this discrimination. Here is a sacred relic. Here we have a thorn from the crown of the world's saviour on whom the prince of this world has no power, which works miracles by its inherent power of the blood shed for us. Thus God himself has chosen this house wherein openly to show forth his power.

It is not men who work these miracles by an unknown and doubtful efficacy, obliging us to a difficult discrimination. It is God himself; it is by the instrument of the passion of his only son, who being present in diverse places, chose this spot and made men come here from all parts to receive miraculous relief of their weakness.

Miracles prove the power which God has over the heart by that which he exerts on the body.

Diverse Thoughts on Religion.

Pyrrhonism is the truth; for, after all, men before Jesus Christ knew not where they were, nor whether they were great or little. And those, who affirmed one or the other, knew nothing about it and only guessed at the reason by chance: yet they always erred in excluding one or the other. *Quod ergo, ignorantes quaeritis, religio annuntiat vobis* (Acts xvii. 23).

The conduct of God, who disposes all things with gentleness, is to put religion in the mind by reasons and in the heart by grace. But to try and put it into the mind and into the heart by force and threatenings, is not to put religion there, but terror, *terrorem potius quam religionem.*

The heart has its reasons which the intellect does not understand; this is seen in a thousand ways. I say that the heart loves the universal Being naturally, and itself naturally, as it gives itself to each and it hardens itself against one or the other at its own will. You have rejected one and reserved the other: is it on rational grounds that you love? It is the heart which feels God, not the reason; that is what constitutes faith: God felt in the heart, not in the intellect.

There are two ways to urge the truth of our religion, one by force of reason, the other by the authority of the speaker. They do not make use of the latter, but of the former. They do not say: You must believe this because Scripture, which says so, is divine, but they say: You must believe it for such and such reasons, a feeble sort of argument, for reason may be turned in every direction.

But even those who seem most opposed to the glory of religion, will not be useless as far as others are concerned. From their case we draw the first argument that there is something supernatural in it; for such blindness is not natural; and if their folly makes them to be so opposed to their own good it may serve to ensure the good of others from horror at an example so deplorable and a folly so worthy of pity.

The ordinary lives of men and of the saints have one thing in common, that both aspire after happiness; they differ as to the object in which they place it. Both call enemies those who prevent their attaining to it. We must judge as to what is good and evil by the will of God, which can be neither unjust nor blind; and not by our own, which is always full of malice and error.

It is a terrible thing to feel all one has passing away!

...Is it *probable* that *probability* will assure us? There is a difference between the sleep and the security of conscience. Nothing gives assurance but truth. Nothing gives rest but the sincere search after truth.

What spoils our comparison of that which happened formerly in the Church and what we see there now is that we usually regard St Athanasius, St Theresa, and the rest as crowned with glory and acting in regard to us as Gods. Now that time has made things clear, it so appears. But at the time when they were persecuted this great saint was a man, who was called Athanasius; and St Theresa a woman. "Elias was a man like ourselves, and subject to like passions as we are," says St James (James v. 17), to disabuse Christians of this false idea which makes us regret the example of the saints as disproportionate to our condition. They were saints, we say, unlike ourselves. What happened at that time? St Athanasius was a man called Athanasius, accused of diverse crimes, condemned in such or such a council, all the bishops consenting, and at last the pope. What say they of those who resisted? That they were disturbers of the peace, that they were schismatics.

Four sorts of persons—zeal without knowledge; knowledge without zeal; neither knowledge nor zeal; and zeal and knowledge. The first three condemn him (i.e. Athanasius), the last acquit him and are excommunicated by the Church, yet save the Church.

Men have a contempt for religion, they hate it and are afraid that it may be true. To cure this we must begin by showing that religion is not contrary to reason; that it is venerable to offer it respect; then to make it liked, make good men hope that it is true, and then show that it is true.

Worthy of veneration, because it has a true knowledge of men; worthy of love, because it promises the true good.

The conditions in which it is most easy to live according to the world are those in which it is most difficult to live according to God; and *vice versâ*. Nothing is so difficult according to the world than the religious life; nothing is more easy according to God. Nothing is more easy than to have an important appointment and ample means according to the world; nothing is more difficult than to live thus according to God, without taking part in or having a taste for them.

The Old Testament contained the types of future joy, and the New Testament the means of obtaining it. The types were of joy; the means penitence; nevertheless the paschal lamb was eaten with bitter herbs (Exod. xii. 8).

PRIDE AND SLOTH, MERCY AND JUSTICE

A person told me one day that he had great joy and confidence in coming out from confession: another told me that he was still fearful. This led me to think that these two together would make one good man, and each was so far wanting in that he had not the feelings of the other. This is often true in other matters.

There is pleasure in being in a vessel beaten about by the storms when we are certain that it will not founder. The persecutions which try the Church are of this nature.

The history of the Church may properly be called the history of truth.

As the two sources of our sins are pride and sloth God has made known to us two of his attributes for their cure: his mercy and his justice. The property of justice is to humble pride, however saintly may be our works, "Enter not into judgment" (Ps. cxliii. 2); and the property of mercy is to combat indolence by exciting to good works, as in the passage: "The goodness of God leadeth thee to repentance" (Rom. ii. 4), and that other of the Ninevites: "Let them turn every one from his evil way, &c." (Jonah iii. 8 sq.). And thus mercy is so far from authorising slackness that, on the contrary, it is the attribute which finally attacks it; so that instead of saying: Were there no mercy with God, we must make every effort after virtue, we should rather say, on the contrary, that because there is mercy in God we must make every effort.

All that is in the world is the lust of the flesh, or the lust of the eye, or the pride of life: *Libido sentiendi; libido sciendi; libido dominandi.* Woe to the accursed land which these three streams of fire inflame rather than moisten! Happy are those who, being on these streams, are plunged in, not carried away by them, but immoveable; firmly fixed above these floods; not standing, but seated and on a base, low and secure, whence they rise not till the day appear; but where, having rested in peace, they stretch forth their hands to him who will lift them up and cause them to stand firm and upright in the porches of the new Jerusalem, where pride can no longer assail and cast them down; and who yet weep, not in seeing the disappearance of perishable things, carried along by the torrents, but at the remembrance of their dear country, the heavenly Jerusalem, which they remember without ceasing during the whole extent of their exile.

The rivers of Babylon flow on, and fall, and sweep along, O holy Zion, where all is stable and where nothing falls!

We must sit upon the streams, not under them, or in them, but on them, not standing but seated; being seated, we are humble; being above them, we are safe. But in the porches of Jerusalem we shall stand.

Let us see if this pleasure is stable, or passing; if passing away, it is a river of Babylon.

Man is so made that by dint of our telling him that he is a fool, he believes it, and by dint of telling it to himself he makes himself believe it; for man holds with himself an inward converse, which requires careful regulation: *Corrumpunt mores bonos colloquia prava* (1 Cor. xv. 33). We must keep silence as much as possible and only hold converse with ourselves about God, whom we know to be the truth: and thus we persuade ourselves of the truth.

Self-will will never be satisfied though it had the power over all it wished, but from the moment that we renounce it we are satisfied. Without it we cannot be discontented; with it we cannot be content.

The true and only virtue, then, is to hate self, for we are hateful on account of lust, and to seek a truly loveable being to love it. But as we cannot love what is outside ourselves we must love a being who is with us, yet is not ourselves, and that is true of all human beings. Now only the universal Being is such. The kingdom of God is within us (Luke xvii. 21). The universal good is

189

within us, in our very self, and yet not ourselves.

It is wrong that people should become attached to me, though they are pleased and willing to do so. I would deceive those in whom I did excite the desire; for I am not the final end of any one, nor have I that which would satisfy them. Am I not about to die? And so the object of their attachment will die. Therefore as I would be guilty of making them believe a falsehood, though I might easily persuade them, and they might believe it with pleasure and in this way give me pleasure; all the same I would be wrong to make myself beloved and to induce people to become attached to me. I must warn those who would be ready to consent to the lie, that they must not believe it, whatever advantage might accrue to me from it: and in the same way that they must not become attached to me; for they ought to spend their life and their pains in pleasing God, or in seeking him.

The trust in form is superstition, but to refuse to submit to them is pride.

There are three means of belief: reason, habit, inspiration. The Christian religion, which alone has reason, does not admit as her true children those who believe without inspiration. Not that she excludes reason and habit; on the contrary, but it is necessary to open the mind to proofs, to confirm ourselves by habit, and then to offer ourselves humbly to inspiration which alone can produce a true and salutary effect: *Ne evacuetur crux Christi* (1 Cor. i. 17).

Men never commit wrong so completely, so gaily as when they do it conscientiously.

Solomon and Job have known best and spoken best of human misery: one the most fortunate, the other most unfortunate; the one knowing by experience the vanity of pleasures, the other the reality of evils.

There are only three sorts of persons: those who serve God, having found him; others, who are engaged in seeking him, not having found him; others, again, who live, not having found him without seeking him. The first are reasonable and happy; the last are foolish and unhappy; those between are unhappy and reasonable.

Reason acts slowly and with so many views, and different principles, which must needs be always present so that at all times it gets drowsy, and goes astray from not having all these principles present. Feeling acts not in this way: it acts instantaneously and is always ready to act. We must, therefore, place our faith in feeling: otherwise it will be always vacillating.

Man is evidently made to think; in this consists his whole dignity, and all his merit; and his whole duty is to think as he ought. Now the order of thought is to begin with self, the author of our being, and our latter end. But what does the world think about? Never of these things; but of dancing, playing the lute, singing, making verses, running at the ring, &c., of fighting, being made king without thinking what it is to be a king and what to be a man.

All the dignity of man is in thought. But what is this thought? How silly it is!

If there is a God, we must love him only and not the creatures of a day. The reasoning of the ungodly in "*the book of wisdom*" (Wisdom ii. 1—9) is only founded on the non-existence of God. This taken for granted, it says: Let us take delight in the creatures, it is the next best thing. But if there were a God to love, this would not be the conclusion arrived at, quite the contrary. And this is the conclusion of the wise: There is a God, let us not, therefore, take delight in the creatures. Hence all that incites us to attach ourselves to the creature is bad; since it hinders us either from serving God if we know him, or from seeking him if we know him not. Now we are full of lust; hence we are full of evil; therefore we ought to hate ourselves and all that which incites us to attach ourselves to anything but God only.

SELF AND SELFLESSNESS

When we try to think about God, is there nothing which turns us away, tempts us to think of other matters? All this is bad, and born with us.

It is false that we are worthy that others should love us; it is unjust that we should wish it. If we were born reasonable, impartial, knowing ourselves and others, we should not impart this bias to our will. However, we are born with it; we are, then, born unjust: for all tends to self. This is contrary to all order: we ought to incline towards the general, and the propensity to self is the beginning of all disorder, in war, in the policy of the state, in economy, in the particular body of man. The will, then, is depraved.

If the members of natural and civil communities incline towards the good of the general body, the communities themselves ought to incline towards another more general body of which they are members. We ought, therefore, to incline towards the general. Therefore we are born unjust and depraved.

Internal war of man between reason and the passions.—If he had only reason without passions....If he had only passions without reason.... But having both, we must have continual war, unable to have peace with one without encountering hostility with the other. Thus man is always divided and at variance with himself.

If it is an unnatural blindness to live without trying to find out what we are, it is a frightful thing to live ill whilst believing in God.

It is beyond doubt that the soul is either mortal or immortal, this should make all the difference in morality; yet philosophers have morality independently of it. They discourse to pass away an hour; Plato to dispose towards Christianity.

The last act is cruel, however lovely the rest of the comedy. At last a little earth is thrown on our head, and there you are for ever.

To regulate the love we owe to ourselves we must imagine a body full of thinking members, for we are members of the whole, and see how each member ought to love itself, &c.

If hands and feet had a will of their own, they would never be in order except by submitting this particular will to the primary will which governs the whole body. Apart from this they are in a state of disorder and unhappy; but in willing only the good of the whole body, they are acting for their own good.

People make an ideal of the truth itself; for truth apart from charity is not God, but his image, an idol, which we must neither love nor worship, and still less must we love and worship its opposite, which is falsehood.

All great distractions are dangerous to the

Christian life; but among all those the world has invented none is more to be feared than the theatre. It is so natural and so delicate a representation of the passions that it excites them and makes them spring up in our heart, above all that of love: principally when it is represented as very chaste and honourable. For the more innocent it appears to innocent souls the more liable are they of being touched by it. Its ardour pleases our self-love, which at once forms the desire of producing the same effects we see so well represented; and we at the same time make it for ourselves a conscience founded on the honour of the sentiments we see there, which removes fear from the poor souls which imagine that no harm can come to purity from loving with a love which appears to them so wise. Thus we leave the theatre with our heart filled with all the beauty and sweetness of love; and the mind and spirit so persuaded of its innocence that we are quite ready to receive its first impressions, or rather to seek for an opportunity of producing them in another's heart that they may receive the same pleasures and the same sacrifices we have seen so well depicted in the theatre.

...Lax opinions please men so much that it is strange that theirs displease them. It is because they exceed all bounds. And moreover there are many people who see the truth and who cannot attain to it. But there are few who do not know that the purity of religion is opposed to our corruptions. It is absurd to say that an eternal recompense is offered for the morality of Escobar.

Silence is the greatest persecution: the saints never held their peace. It is true we must have a call, but it is not from the orders of the council that we must learn that we are called, it is from the necessity of speaking. But after Rome has spoken, and men think that she condemned the truth, and they have written it, and that the books, which have contradicted it, are censured, we must cry so much the louder, the more unjustly we are censured and the more violently they try to stifle speech, until there come a pope, who hears both sides and who consults antiquity to do justice. So good popes will still find the Church in an uproar.

...The inquisition and the society of Jesuits the two scourges of truth.

...Why do you not accuse them of Arianism? For if they have said that Jesus Christ is God, perhaps it is not in its natural meaning they understand him, but as it is said: *Dii estis* (Ps. lxxxii. 6).

If my letters are condemned in Rome what I condemn in them is condemned in heaven: *Ad tuum, domine Jesu, tribunal appello.*

POVERTY AND WEALTH

You yourself are corruptible. I was afraid that I had written badly, seeing myself condemned, but the example of so many pious writings made me believe the contrary. It is no longer permitted to write well, so corrupt and ignorant is the inquisition!

It is better to obey God rather than men (Acts v. 29).

...I am afraid of nothing, I hope nothing. Not so with the Bishops. Port Royal is afraid, and it is bad policy to disperse them for they will no longer fear, but make themselves feared the more. I do not even fear your censures of this kind unless they are founded on those of tradition. So you censure all? What, even my respect? No. Then tell me what it is, or you will do nothing since you do not point out the evil, and why it is evil, and this they will find difficult to do.

I love poverty because he loved it. I love wealth because it affords us the means of assisting the unfortunate. I keep faith with all. I do not return evil to those who wrong me, but I wish them to have a condition like mine in which we receive neither good nor evil from men. I try to be just, true, sincere, or faithful to all men, and have a tenderness of heart for those to whom God has more closely united me...and whether I am alone, or seen of men, I do all my actions in the sight of God, who must judge them and to whom I have consecrated them. Such are my sentiments; and I bless every day of my life my redeemer, who has put them in me, and who, of a man full of weaknesses, unhappiness, lust, pride, and ambition, has made one exempt of all these evils by the power of his grace, to which all the glory of it is due, having nothing in myself except misery and error.

Nature has perfections to show that she is the image of God; and imperfections to show that it is only the image.

Men are of necessity such fools that it would be playing the fool by another turn of folly trying not to be a fool.

To make a man a saint, grace, indeed, is necessary: and whosoever doubts about it does not know what a saint, or a man is. Everything can be fatal to our existence, even things made to serve us; as in nature walls can kill us, and stairs can kill us if we do not walk circumspectly.

The least movement affects all nature. The entire sea changes for a stone. So is grace, the least action by its consequences is important to the whole. Therefore everything is important.

In each action we must look beyond the action at our present, past, and future state, and to others to whom it is important, and to see the connection of all these things. And then we shall be very cautious.

Man is not worthy of God, but he is not incapable to render himself worthy of him.

It is unworthy of God to join himself to a miserable man, but it is not unworthy of God to draw him out of his misery.

Eloquence is the art of saying things in such a fashion (1) that those to whom we speak can hear it without pain and with pleasure; (2) that they feel interested so that self-love leads them more willingly to reflect upon it. It consists, then, in the correspondence we try to establish between the mind and the heart of those whom we address, on the one hand, and the thoughts and expressions we employ, on the other; this supposes that we have made a thorough study of the human heart in order to know all its springs, and then to find the true proportion of the discourse we try to adapt to it. We must put ourselves in the place of the hearers and try on our own heart the turns we give to our discourse, to see that they suit each other, so as to make sure that the hearers will be, as it were, compelled to surrender. We must confine ourselves, as far as possible, to what is simple and natural; not to magnify what is small, nor belittle what is great. It is not that the thing should be beautiful, it must be appropriate to the subject, that there be nothing redundant and nothing deficient.

Eloquence is a painting of thought; and thus those, who, after having painted it, add somewhat more, make a picture in place of a portrait.

If we ought to do nothing save on a certainty, we ought to do nothing for religion; for this is not of a certain nature. But how much we do on an uncertainty, sea-voyages, battles! Therefore I say we ought to do nothing at all, for nothing is certain; and that there is more certainty in religion than there is that we shall see another day: for it is not certain that we shall see to-morrow, but it is certainly possible that we shall not see it. We cannot say thus much of religion. It is not certain that it is (true); but who dares to say that it is certainly possible that it is not? But when we work for to-morrow and for what is uncertain we act reasonably. For we should work for the uncertain by the doctrine of chances which was demonstrated above.

We must have a thought at the background and judge all this and yet speak like the rest of the world.

Force is the queen of the world, and not opinion: but opinion is that which makes use of force.

FORCE AND PROGRESS

Force creates opinion. Gentleness is beautiful according to our opinion. Why? For he who would dance on a rope will stand alone (in his task), and I will get a larger crowd of people, who will say that it is unbecoming.

Everything which is perfected by progress perishes, also, with progress. All that was feeble cannot become absolutely strong. It is vain to say: He has grown, he has changed, he is still the same.

Atheists ought to say what is perfectly evident, but it is not perfectly evident that the soul is material.

Unbelievers are most credulous. They believe in the miracles of Vespasian in order not to believe in those wrought by Moses.

Atheism is a mark of strength of mind, yet only to a certain extent.

Desires and Christian Duties.

When our passions carry us away to any act we forget our duty. If we like a book we read it when we ought to do something else. But, as a reminder, we ought to propose to ourselves a task we dislike; we then make excuses that we have something else to do and so remember our duty.

What distortion of the judgment by which

everybody puts himself above all the rest of the world, and prefers his own well-being and the duration of his happiness, or his life, to that of all the rest!

We not only look at things from different sides, but with different eyes; we do not care to find them alike.

Our nature consists in movement; complete repose is death.

We know ourselves so little, that many think they are going to die when they are well, and some think they are well when they are on the point of death, not feeling the approaching fever, or the abscess ready to form.

It is not our own power which sustains our virtue, but the counterpoise of two opposite vices; we remain standing as between two contrary winds; remove one of these vices and we fall into the other.

Memory is necessary to all the operations of reason.

Instinct and reason, marks of two natures.

When I consider the short duration of my life, swallowed up in the eternity which goes before and follows after; the small space I occupy, or even can see, engulfed in the infinite immensity of spaces which I ignore, and which ignore me; I am filled with fear and astonishment to see myself here rather than there, for there is no reason whatever why either here or there, why now rather than afterwards. Who has placed me there? By whose order, and by whose management has the place and time been destined to me? *Memoria hospitis unius diei praetereuntis* (Wisdom v. 14).

Why is my knowledge limited? My stature? The duration of my life to a hundred rather than a thousand? What reason had nature for giving me such a life, for choosing this number rather than another, in the infinity of those for which there is no reason for choosing one rather than another, nothing tending one way or another?

The eternal silence of infinite spaces terrifies me. Everyone is a whole to himself; for when dead all is dead for him.

Ordinary people have the power of not thinking about what they do not like to think. Do not think about the passages concerning the Messiah, said a Jew to his son. Our people do often the same. In this way false religions are preserved! Even the true with regard to other people. But those who have not the power of thus preventing thought, and who think all the more it is forbidden them—these shake off false religions and even the true unless they find solid arguments.

How far is the knowledge of God from the love of God!

Nothing is so intolerable to man than to be in complete rest without passions, without business, without amusement, without application. He thus feels his nothingness, his loneliness, his insufficiency, his dependence, his impotence, his emptiness. There will arise immediately from the depth of his soul weariness, gloominess, sadness, sorrow, contempt, and despair.

Man does nothing by reason, although it is the essence of his existence.

All their principles are true, those of the sceptics, Stoics, atheists, &c. But their conclusions are false, because the opposite principles are, also, true.

We owe much to those who point out faults, for they mortify us. They teach us that we have been despised, they do not prevent our being so in future, for we have many other faults to bring this about. They only prepare the way for discipline of correction and freedom from fault.

Faith is the gift of God: do not think that we said that it is the gift of reason. Other religions do not say this of their faith; they only offer reason to arrive at it and yet it never leads to it.

Such figures of the redemption of all, as that of the sun shining upon all, point only to the whole;

but those about exclusions, as of the Jews elected to the exclusion of the Gentiles, point to exclusion.

"Jesus Christ, redeemer of all."—Yes, he has offered like a man who redeemed all who are willing to come to him: as for those who shall die on the way, that is their misfortune; but as for him, he has offered them redemption.—This holds good in the case in which he who redeems and preserves from death are two, but not in Jesus Christ, who has done one and the other.— No, for Jesus Christ, in his capacity as redeemer, is not, perhaps, master of all; and thus so far as it is in him, he is the redeemer of all.

It is no rare thing to have to reprove the world for too much docility; it is a vice as natural as incredulity and equally pernicious. Superstition.

There are few true Christians, I say this even in regard to faith. There are many who believe, but from superstition; there are many who do not believe, but from evil living: few there are between the two.

I do not include here those whose morality is the true piety, and all those who believe by a sentiment of the heart.

Our religion is wise and foolish. Wise, because it is the most learned and the one most founded on miracles, prophecies, &c. Foolish, because it is not all this which causes us to belong to it; it may well condemn those who are not of it, but it does not make those believe who are. What makes them believe is the Cross, *ne evacuata sit crux*. And thus St Paul, who came with wisdom and signs, says that he had not come with wisdom and signs, for he came to convert. But those who only come to convince may say that they come in wisdom and signs.

We must know ourselves : if this does not serve to discover truth, it, at least, serves to regulate our life, and there is nothing more just.

When we would pursue the virtues to their extremes, at either side vices appear which sensibly insinuate themselves there in their insensible course from the side of the infinitely little; and vices appear in plenty on the side of the infinitely great, in such a way that we lose ourselves in the vices and no longer see the virtues (we find fault with perfection itself).

From our infancy admiration spoils everything. Oh! how well expressed! Oh! how well done! how clever he is! &c. The children of Port Royal, to whom we do not offer the spur of emulation and glory, fall into carelessness.

Experience shows us a vast difference between devoutness and goodness.

We do not weary of eating and sleeping every

day, for hunger and sleepiness recur; but for that we should weary of them. So without hunger for spiritual things we get weary of them. Hunger after righteousness, the eighth beatitude.

There are only two kinds of men: the righteous, who believe themselves sinners, and the rest sinners, who believe themselves righteous.

It is not good to have too much liberty. It is not good to have all we want.

It is impossible that God should be always the end if he is not the beginning. We look upwards, but cling to the dust; and the earth gives way and we fall, gazing up to heaven.

All is one, all is different. How many natures exist in man! How many vocations! And by what chance does each man ordinarily accept what he has heard praised?

Description of man: dependency, desire of independence, want.

Wisdom sends us to childhood: *Nisi efficiamini sicut parvuli* (Mat. xviii. 3).

True religion teaches us our duties, our weaknesses (pride and concupiscence) and the remedies (humility, mortification). Men must be sincere in all religions: true pagans, true Jews, true Christians.

All that God does not wish is forbidden. Sins are forbidden by a general declaration made by God that he will not have them. Other things, which he has left without a general prohibition, and of which for that reason we say that they are permitted, are nevertheless, not always permitted. For when God removes one of these from us, and it appears by the event, which is a manifestation of the will of God, that he does not wish us to have something, it is then forbidden like a sin, since it is the will of God that we should have neither one nor the other. There is only this difference between the two, that it is certain that God in no case permits sin, whereas it is not so as to whether he will never have the other. But so long as God does not wish it, we must regard it as sin; so long as the absence of the will of God, which alone is all goodness and all justice, renders it unjust and evil.

The arrangement by dialogue.—What ought I to do? I see only obscurity everywhere. Shall I believe that I am nothing? Shall I believe that I am God? All things change and succeed one another. You are mistaken, there is....

If God had given us masters under his own hand, Oh! how we ought to obey them with all our heart! necessity and events are infallibly such.

These people lack heart, do not make friends of them.

We think we play a common organ when we

touch men. They are organs, indeed, but odd ones, changeable, variable. Those who can only touch ordinary organs will not produce harmony out of these. We must know where the pipes are.

Reasons seen from a distance seem to limit our view, when they are realised they no longer do so; we begin to see beyond.

External works. There is nothing so dangerous as that which pleases both God and men. For those conditions, which are pleasing alike to God and men, are those when one thing pleases God, and another pleases men, as the greatness of St Theresa: what pleases God is her profound humility in her revelations; what pleases men are her illuminations. And so we torment ourselves to imitate her sayings, thinking to imitate her condition; and not so much to love that which God loves, and put ourselves into that which God loves.

True Christianity consists in submission of reason and its use.

That we must love one God only is a thing so evident that no miracles are required to prove it.

This religion so great in miracles (holy and blameless fathers, scholars, and great men, witnesses, martyrs, established kings; (David) Isaiah, prince of the blood), so great in knowledge, after

having displayed all these miracles and all this
wisdom, rejects all that and says that there is
neither wisdom nor signs, but the Cross and
foolishness. For those who by these signs and
by this wisdom have merited belief, and have
proved their character, declare to you that none
of these things can change you, or render us
capable to know and love God except the virtue
of the foolishness of the Cross, without wisdom
or signs; and not the signs without the power.

Thus our religion is foolish as regards the
efficient cause, wise as regards the wisdom which
prepares the way for it.

Augustine, *de Civ.* v. 10. This rule is universal.
God can do all except the things which, if he
were capable of doing them, he would not be all-
powerful, such as die, be deceived, lie, &c.

The Mystery of Jesus.

Jesus suffers in his passion those torments
which men have inflicted on him; but in the
agony he suffers the torments which he inflicts
on himself: *turbare semetipsum* (John xi. 33). It
is a punishment from a hand, not human but all-
powerful, for to sustain it needs omnipotence.

Jesus seeks some comfort, at least, in three
dearest friends, and they sleep. He prays them

to endure with him a while (Mat. xxvi. 38), and they leave him with complete neglect, having so little compassion that it could not even prevent them from sleeping for a moment. And thus Jesus was left alone to the wrath of God.

Jesus was without one on earth to feel and share his suffering, but even to know of it, he and heaven were alone in that knowledge.

Jesus is in a garden, not of delights like the first Adam, where he ruined himself and the whole human race; but of pains in which he was saved and the whole human race.

He suffers this pain and desertion in the horror of the night.

I believe that Jesus never complained but this once only; but then he complains as if he could no longer contain his excessive pain: My soul is sorrowful even unto death.

Jesus seeks companionship and consolation from men. This was the only time in his life, as it seems to me. But he does not receive it, for his disciples were asleep.

Jesus will be in agony to the end of the world: we must not sleep all the while.

Jesus in the midst of this universal desertion and that of his friends, chosen to watch with him, finding them sleeping, is sorry for it on account of the danger to which they, not he, are exposed, and reminds them of their own safety and good, with a heartfelt tenderness for them in their ingratitude, and warns them that the spirit is willing, but the flesh is weak.

Jesus, still finding them sleeping, unrestrained by any consideration for themselves, or himself, had the kindness not to wake them, and leaves them to their repose.

Jesus prays, uncertain of the will of his Father, and fears death; but, as soon as he knows it, he goes forth to give himself up to it:—*Eamus. Processit* (John xviii. 4).

Jesus besought men, but was not heard.

Jesus, whilst his disciples slept, wrought their salvation. He wrought that of all the just whilst they slept, both in their nothingness before their birth, in the sins since their birth.

He only prays once that the cup may pass away, and yet with submission, and twice that it may come if it be necessary.

Jesus in weariness. Jesus, seeing all his friends asleep and all his enemies wakeful, gives himself over entirely to his Father.

Jesus does not regard in Judas his enmity, but the bidding of God, which he loves and admits, since he calls him friend.

Jesus tears himself away from his friends to enter into his glory. We ought to tear ourselves away from our nearest and most intimate friends to imitate him.

Jesus, being in an agony and in the greatest sufferings, let us pray longer (Luke xxii. 44).

Console thyself: thou wouldest not seek, hadst thou not found me.

I thought of thee in my agony; I have shed so many tears of blood for thee.

It is tempting me rather than proving thyself, to think whether thou couldest act well in a case which has not occurred; I will act in thee if it occur.

Let my rules guide thee, see how well I have guided the virgin and the saints, who let me act in them.

The father loves all *I* do.

Shall I for ever shed my human blood, thou shedding no tears?

Thy conversion is my affair, fear nothing and pray with confidence; as for me, I am present with thee by my word in Scripture, by my spirit in the Church, and by inspirations; by my power in the priests, by my prayer among the faithful.

The doctors will not heal thee, for thou wilt die at last. But it is I who make the body immortal.

Suffer chains and bodily servitude; I deliver thee now only from spiritual servitude.

I am thy friend more than any one; for I have done for thee more than they, and they would not suffer what I have suffered for thee, they would not die for thee in the days of thine infidelities and cruelties, as I have done, and am ready to do, and do in mine elect and in the holy sacrament.

If thou knewedst thy sins thou wouldest lose heart.—I shall lose it, then, Lord, for on thy word I believe their malice.—No, for I by whom thou learnest it can heal them and what I tell thee is a sign that I will heal thee. As thou dost expiate them, thou wilt know them and it will be said to thee: "Behold, thy sins are forgiven thee." Repent, then, for thy secret sins and for the hidden malice of those which thou knowest.—Lord, I give thee all.—

I love thee more ardently than thou hast loved thy impurities. *Ut immundus pro luto.*

That to me be the glory, not to thee, worm and dust.

Consult thy director when my own words are to thee an occasion of evil, or vanity, or curiosity.

I see the depth in me of pride, curiosity, lust. There is no relation between me and God, or Jesus Christ, the Just One. But he has been made sin for me, all thy plagues are fallen upon him. He is more abominable than I, and far from abhorring me, he holds himself honoured that I go to him, and succour him.

But he has healed himself and with greater reason will heal me.

I must add my plagues to his and join myself to him and he will save me in saving himself.

But there must be no adding to them in the future.

Console thyself: it is not from you that you must expect it; but, on the contrary, by expecting nothing from yourself you must await it.

Jesus Christ was dead, but seen, on the Cross, he is dead and hidden in the sepulchre.

Jesus Christ was buried by the saints alone, Jesus Christ worked no miracles at the sepulchre.

The saints alone entered it.

There, not on the Cross, Jesus Christ takes a new life.

It is the last mystery of passion and re-demption.

Jesus Christ had nowhere where to rest on the earth but in the tomb.

His enemies only ceased to persecute him at the tomb.

I speak to thee and often advise thee, because thy director cannot speak to thee; for I do not wish thee to be without director. And perhaps I grant it to his prayers, thus he leads thee without thou seeing him. Thou wouldest not seek me if thou didst not possess me. Be not anxious, then, compare not thyself with others, but with me. If thou findest me not in those with whom thou comparest thyself, thou comparest thyself with one that is abominable. If thou findest me there, compare thyself to me. But whom wilt thou compare? Thyself, or me in thee? If it be thyself it is one that is abominable. If it be me thou comparest me with myself. Now I am God in all.

It seems to me that Jesus Christ only allowed his wounds to be touched after his resurrection: *Noli me tangere* (John xx. 17). We may only be one with him in his sufferings.

He has given himself in communion as one about to die, in the supper, to his disciples, as one risen, at Emmaus, to the whole Church, as one ascended into heaven.

" Pray that ye enter not into temptation " (Luke xxii. 46). It is dangerous to be tempted; and those alone are tempted who do not pray.

Et tu conversus confirma fratres tuos (Luke xxii. 32). But before that *conversus Jesus respexit Petrum* (Luke xxii. 61).

St Peter asked permission to strike Malchus, and strikes before having the answer; Jesus answered afterwards.

Jesus Christ did not wish to be killed without the legal forms; for it is more ignominious to die by justice than by unjust sedition.

The false justice of Pilate only serves to make Jesus suffer, for he has him scourged by a false justice and then slays him. He should have slain him at the first. Thus it is with those who are falsely just. They do good and evil works to please the world and show that they are not altogether of Jesus Christ; for they are ashamed of him. Then, at last, in great temptations and on great occasions, they slay him.

Pascal's Confession of Faith.

Found after his death sewn in his doublet, apparently indicating the definite moment of his final conversion.

The Year of Grace, 1654.

Monday, November 23rd, day of St Clement, Pope and Martyr, and others in the Martyrology. Eve of St Chrysogonus, martyr, and others.

From about half past ten at night to about half past twelve.

Fire.

God of Abraham, God of Isaac, God of Jacob. Not of the Philosophers and the men of Science. Certainty, Certainty, Feeling, Joy, Peace.

God of Jesus Christ.

Deum meum et Deum vestrum.
Thy God shall be my God.

Forgetfulness of the world and of all apart from God.

He can be found only by the ways taught in the Gospel.

Greatness of the human soul.

O righteous Father, the world has not known thee, but I have known thee.

Joy, Joy, Joy, tears of Joy.

I have separated myself from him.

Dereliquerunt me fontem aquae vivae.

Wilt thou leave me, O my God?

May I not be separated from him for ever.

This is life eternal that they may know thee the only true God and Jesus Christ whom thou hast sent.

Jesus Christ.
Jesus Christ.

NOTHING SHALL SEPARATE

I have separated myself from him; I have fled, renounced, crucified him.

May I never be separated from him.

He maintains himself in me only in the ways taught in the Gospel.

Renunciation total and sweet, &c.

NOTES

p. 59, l. 9. *Gentleman.* It is not easy to render into English *honnête homme.* Some translate " honourable man," others "upright man"; but the term honnêteté (der. from Latin honestus and honestas), as used by Montaigne and writers of the 17th century, means more than this, namely what we understand and cannot easily define, i.e. gentlemanly bearing and conduct.

p. 62, l. 26. *Why should I divide my morality into four parts,* &c., refers to the classic division of moral philosophy into Justice, Fortitude, Prudence, and Temperance, the four cardinal virtues.

p. 66, l. 1. *The Divisions of Charron, which sadden and weary,* &c., refers to his *Traité de la sagesse,* containing 117 chapters with many subdivisions.

p. 80, l. 2. *Salomon de Tultie.* A pseudonym, like Louis de Montalte, the professed author of the *Provincial Letters,* standing for Pascal himself.

p. 93, l. 21. *Des Barreaux,* a contemporary of Pascal (b. 1602, d. 1673), well-known for his Epicureanism, but also for his fits of repentance and devotion when overtaken by illness. Balzac calls him the "new Bacchus"; Bayle says of him, "En santé c'était un homme d'un libertinage outré; malade il faisait de sonnets dévots."

p. 108, l. 7. *That men,* &c. Here the author

NOTES

breaks off, as in a number of other passages, leaving out the rest for further elaboration, e.g. on p. 113 and again on p. 208, and passim.

p. 108, l. 16. *The error of this dilemma in Montaigne* refers to a passage in the Essays of Montaigne, Bk II. Ch. xii., where he speaks of the following dilemma of the philosophers: "The soul is either mortal, or immortal; if mortal, it will suffer no pain; if immortal, it will change for the better." "They never touch," Montaigne goes on to say, "the other branch: what of the change for the worse?"

p. 117, l. 13. *The void does not exist.* The argument here referred to is found in the treatise of Grotius, *De Veritate*, Bk I. Ch. vii, about nature abhorring a vacuum, which Pascal was one of the first to discard as a scientific theory.

p. 118, l. 2. *The automaton.* The idea is here of automatic action as distinguished from that which results from a process of reason, in accordance with the Cartesian philosophy. Descartes, indeed, regarded animals as automata, machines without intellect or emotion, and Pascal on this point agreed with him.

p. 141, l. 20. *My heart entirely inclines me*, &c. This sentence, observes Voltaire, is an imitation from Corneille's *Héraclius* (Act IV. Sc. iv.):

Que veux-tu donc, nature, et que prétends-tu faire?
De quoi parle à mon coeur ton murmure imparfait?
Ne me dis rien du tout, ou parle tout-à-fait;

and speaks of it as the best of the *Pensées*.

p. 143, l. 17. *The law of the XII. Tables.* Probably
a quotation from Grotius, loc. cit. I. xv, "Sicut et
antiquissimae leges Atticae, unde et romanae postea
desumptae ex legibus Moisis originem ducunt."

p. 160, l. 20. *It would have been useless for
Archimedes to play the Prince.* As a matter of fact
Archimedes was related to King Hiero (Plutarch), but
the latter, simply τύραννος of a Greek city, as M. Havet
points out, scarcely ranked with "prince" as then understood. Cicero speaks of him as an obscure man apart
from his geometry : "Humilem homunculum a pulvere
et radio excitabo" (*Tusc.* v. 23).

p. 176, l. 16. *Thoughts on Miracles.* These form
really the starting-point of what was intended to be
Pascal's *Apologia*, for the basis of the reasoning was
the miraculous cure of Pascal's niece, Marguerite Périer,
an inmate of Port Royal, of an eye complaint by the
relic of the Holy Thorn. This deeply impressed Pascal, but the authenticity of the miracle was called in
question by the Jesuits.

p. 188, l. 24. *The rivers of Babylon.* This is
taken from St Augustine's paraphrase of Psalm cxxxvi.,
"Super flumina Babylonis." Babylon is the world;
Sion is Heaven. The rivers of Babylon are the temptations of life.

p. 195, l. 25. *Theatre.* The reflections on the
theatre are not in the Autograph MS., but in the copy.
They were first published by Bossut in 1779.

p. 196, l. 5. *Morality of Escobar.* Antonio
Escobar of Mendoza was the author of the system of

morality, which Pascal so severely condemns in the
5th and 6th of the *Provincial Letters* on account of the
equivocations it contains.

p. 201, l. 4. *Get a larger crowd.* The original
here is " Je ferai une cabale plus forte." This Mr C.
Kegan Paul translates "A stronger cabal of people,"
but that does not convey a very distinct idea to English
readers. Evidently Pascal means that he could get a
larger number of people to disapprove of a startling
public exhibition, but there is some little obscurity in
the peculiar wording.

p. 210, l. 17. *The Mystery of Jesus.* This fragment
was first discovered by Faugère, who found it on p. 87
of the Autograph.

p. 214, l. 19. *Ut immundus pro luto.* A mis-
quotation, possibly a reminiscence of 2 Pet. ii. 22,
" Sus lota in volutabro luti."

p. 219. The copy of the parchment on which this
confession of faith is written contained in addition the
following words:

Total submission to Jesus Christ and my director.
For ever in joy in return for one day's toil on earth.
Non obliviscar sermones tuos. Amen.

INDEX.

INDEX

INDEX

228

INDEX

For EU product safety concerns, contact us at Calle de José Abascal, 56–1°,
28003 Madrid, Spain or eugpsr@cambridge.org.

www.ingramcontent.com/pod-product-compliance
Ingram Content Group UK Ltd.
Pitfield, Milton Keynes, MK11 3LW, UK
UKHW012331130625
459647UK00009B/200